TOGETHER
IS
HOME

Together Is Home

The Healing Messages of
A COURSE IN MIRACLES

Lara Pollock

TOGETHER IS HOME PUBLICATIONS

WICHITA, KANSAS

Table of Contents

*This book is dedicated to anyone
who has ever wondered*
WHY?

PREFACE

THERE have been many clues in my life indicating that I would write a book at some point. I have always loved stories, theater, word play, and writing in general. However, I've spent most of my life involved in all kinds of activities. Once my husband and I raised our kids, more time became available, but I just didn't prioritize writing a book at that point.

When the Covid-19 pandemic unfolded, many changes fell into place. I closed my practice in Chinese Medicine to stay home and care for my mother who is in her 90's. This situation presented much more opportunity to write, though the idea of self-publishing a book did not yet seem achievable.

Early on, when the book was an amorphous 'maybe' my mom gave me the nudge to see this project through. She and I were admiring her bookshelf where we've displayed a book published by my grandmother, *Jump the Rope Jingles*, as well as Mom's meditation book, *Tree and Jubilee*. She said, "Maybe someday your book will sit up there, too." As I pondered this, a vibration went through me. It felt like an opening up, a vision and a decision all at the same time. Then I knew a third-generation volume would be taking its place on her bookshelf.

A few months later, in January 2022, I began writing about the basic concepts of *A Course in Miracles*. My Calling was clear, my vision for the book never wavered: Streamline and explain the most basic concepts to help people better understand the Course's profound wisdom teachings.

Completing the book has taken deep commitment and follow-through. My writing process is not a quick and easy one—what should take twenty minutes tends to take two hours. There were times when I was unsure how to proceed, yet each step has been guided, each aspect has fallen into place exactly as it should.

For example, here's a little story about the book's title. A few years ago I was running errands and I pulled up to a mini-mall. I felt prompted to go into a shop I hadn't noticed before. There were various trendy items in the store, but I don't decorate according to trends—I just get things that I find beautiful, then look for a place to put them.

Even though I couldn't find anything that appealed to me at the little shop, I wanted to support the local business by buying something. I knew I had been pulled there for a reason, so I Asked Spirit, "Please show me what I am here to see." My eyes fell on a plaque, about a foot long, with three simple words on it, "Together Is Home." I loved it! I knew this was it, and the sign promptly went onto the mantel in our family room.

When I first began writing, I was typing away and then I paused to ponder what the title of this book might be. I Asked Spirit, "Do we have a title yet?" As I looked up, my eyes landed on the plaque sitting on the mantel—Together Is Home. Ah Yes, we do have a title, and Thank You, Spirit. Thank You very much!

I am so grateful for Spirit's guidance each step of the way, and that's the only way I ever want it to be. May you connect with this same guidance as you explore these pages. I can think of no better way to spend time than learning and sharing the healing messages of *A Course in Miracles*.

~ Lara Pollock

CHAPTER 1

Discovering *A Course in Miracles*

MANY years ago, my dear Aunt Nancy shared her definition of obsession with me. It was when she was managing her own all-consuming fascination with the Terra Cotta Warriors, which were discovered near Xi'an, China in 1974. Aunt Nancy laughed and said, "If it's the first thing you think about when you wake up, and the last thing you think about when you go to sleep, that's an obsession!" By her definition, and by most other commonly-recognized criteria, I am obsessed with *A Course in Miracles*!

I have been a seeker all my life, wandering, wondering, searching, and questioning: WHY? Until finding *A Course in Miracles*, I continuously grappled with the question: "What is going on with this messed-up world? It does not make sense." The lame response is, "Well, that's just the way of the world." Then people go about their business pretending it *does* make sense.

Perhaps you have questioned this as well? WHY do we struggle and strive to attain, yet eventually lose everything? WHY do we tolerate living with uncertainty, corruption, and conflict? It does not feel right, and it never has. If God is perfect and if God created the world, WHY is this world so glaringly imperfect? It does not make sense.

When I was growing up, I would sometimes experience an eerie identity crisis when I looked in the mirror. I had this knowing that the unseen world was more real than this world. It was unsettling because it reminded me that I didn't want to be in this false-feeling place. It started as a sinking sensation, then dizzying waves of 'not-right-ness' washed over me. As I looked in the mirror, a nagging feeling kept telling me this is not who I Am. Who is this person in the mirror?—Because it is not me! I wanted to escape the image reflecting back at me. Eventually, these disturbing episodes ebbed, but I still never accepted the authenticity of "the way of the world."

From my teenage years on, these incongruent feelings generated confusion and existential angst. Being highly sensitive, living in this wrong-feeling realm was such a struggle at times. If I couldn't understand what the point of all this was, I was not fully committed to enduring it. This is what prompted my persistent search to find out WHY.

In my twenties and thirties, this search included reading a wide variety of books. Examples of the many books I read, in hopes of finding definitive answers, include: The Bible, *There Is A River*, *Science of Mind*, *The Celestine Prophecy*, *Zen Physics*, *Holographic Universe*, *The Journey of Souls*, *The Power of Now*, and many others. [See Appendix: Perspectives on Study Methods & Recommended Reading List.] Each of these books lent new insights for me, helping me to understand the world in a new light. Yet none of them provided me with a comprehensive answer for, "WHY is there so much suffering in this world? And WHY are we here?"

The turning point came in 2007, when a friend mentioned *The Disappearance of the Universe* (DU) by Gary Renard. Remarkably, the random mention of this book completely changed the course of my life. This is because DU explains the significance of the Love-based wisdom teaching, *A Course in Miracles* (ACIM). This discovery has transformed my life in miraculous ways. There simply are not words to convey the depth of meaning it has for me. Within the Course, I have finally found a comprehensive answer to: WHY?

ACIM Background

A Course in Miracles is a spiritual self-study curriculum that was scribed in the 1960's and 70's by two psychologists at Columbia University, Dr. Helen Schucman and Dr. Bill Thetford. There are numerous resources describing the development of this timeless wisdom teaching and I recommend starting with the website *acim.org* for the Foundation for Inner Peace (FIP) which was co-founded by Judith Skutch Whitson. Additionally, *Absence from Felicity* by Kenneth Wapnick includes fascinating details of Helen's life and the development of the Course. Carol Howe's biography of Bill Thetford, *Never Forget to Laugh*, is one of my favorite books. Though there are different perspectives between these two books, I recommend them both if you are interested in learning about the scribes of *A Course in Miracles.*

The scribing of the Course began in 1965. Helen started to receive compelling messages shortly after Bill expressed his frustration with the competitive hostilities between their colleagues. It was a particularly difficult day, and Bill made an impassioned speech to Helen, concluding with the emphatic statement, "There must be another way." Helen agreed with Bill, and she made a definitive decision to help him find this better way. Shortly afterwards, she began to receive powerful visions and dreams. This upset her greatly, but Bill encouraged her to continue writing down everything she was experiencing. One night in October 1965, Helen heard a Voice tell her, in the form of inner dictation, "This is a course in miracles. Please take notes."

Helen was often anxious, and this pattern increased while she was beginning to scribe the Course. Here she was, a self-proclaimed atheist, hearing a mysterious Voice! It is certainly understandable that both Helen and Bill were concerned for their reputations as leading professors in the field of psychology.

Every morning, she read from her shorthand notes and Bill transcribed what she relayed to him. At times, scribing the content was too upsetting for Helen's atheistic mindset, so she would try to ignore the inner dictation. One reason Helen was so anxious is because it was evident that the messages were coming from the Voice of Yeshua, also known as, Jesus. She was terribly resistant to this, and we would not have the Course today if Bill had not continuously encouraged her throughout the process. It took seven years for them to complete the writings, with a few additions coming through after that. Finally, the first edition of *A Course in Miracles* was published by The Foundation for Inner Peace in 1976.

A Framework for Understanding

I have studied the Course since 2008 and I am still building bridges of understanding as I apply its healing thought system every single day. It is a living document in the sense that every time I go back and read the same words, the meaning speaks to me at a deeper level.

At first, however, ACIM's concepts can be quite difficult to grasp. It is usually best to take it slowly, learning the basics first. With this in mind, there are some Course terms and concepts that will not be deeply explored in this book. My intention here is to introduce the basic concepts that are foundational to the Course. Though these basics are also difficult to explain, I hope to provide a framework, a trellis upon which the vines of your own understanding will grow and bloom.

I feel it is helpful to have companion resources to explain the Course's important messages. If a person were to just pick up ACIM and dive right in, honestly, it might not go so well. Many people purchase the book, try to read it, then toss it on the bookshelf where it sits for years. If there is no companion book to help navigate the Course, it can be overwhelming and off-putting. For example, when I began studying ACIM, I struggled significantly with the use of masculine pronouns and biblical terminology. I certainly would not have continued reading the Course without constant reinforcement from *The Disappearance of the Universe.*

Another impediment to studying the Course is that complicated concepts are being introduced from the very beginning. A companion book, like this one or DU, helps students make sense of what the Course is saying. One vital concept that companion books clarify is ACIM's approach to forgiveness, which is much different than how the world defines it. True Forgiveness is the key concept for every aspect of the Course, and this will be further explained as we go along.

There are many books designed to simplify the Course;

what I share here may or may not coincide with those approaches. Some of what I share could be controversial, as there is a wide spectrum of opinions on the messages of the Course. I am aligned with teacher David Hoffmeister's perspective, which is for each student to use whatever they have been guided to use for their individualized curriculum. If an ACIM resource feels helpful, then use that approach. You can gauge when you are on the right track by how you feel. The more you tune in to how you are feeling in the moment, the more you will know if you are following your individualized curriculum.

The vision for *Together Is Home* is to give a step-by-step, progressive explanation of WHY we are experiencing this world which seems to be separate from God. That said, ACIM concepts are often not meant to be understood intellectually. The meaning emerges in your mind as you take time to read, learn and apply these wisdom teachings to your own life circumstances.

CHAPTER 2

Preparing to Read ACIM

Ask Spirit, Pause & Listen—This is my first recommendation for reading *A Course in Miracles*. The term 'Spirit' refers specifically to the Holy Spirit, described as the Voice for God in ACIM. In my daily Asking, I refer to the Holy Spirit or Spirit interchangeably. The idea is to turn within to your own intuitive connection. Some people prefer to call on Yeshua or Jesus; others are more comfortable relying on God, Higher Self, Divine Love, or Mother Mary as their go-to support system. Any of these conceptualizations works wonderfully to connect with the support of a powerful inner resource.

Every day I gain more appreciation for the guidance available to us in every aspect of life. When studying ACIM, I am often impressed with how powerful it is to 'Ask Spirit' to read with me—the words come alive and speak to me! Spirit's gentle guidance is always available, though when we Ask Spirit, Pause & Listen, it is even more effective. This is because Spirit does not impose on us. We have access to great resources when we invite assistance. Asking can be as simple as, "Spirit, help." Many times, I simply say "Spirit" with the intention of receiving the messages that are right for each situation.

It can be even more helpful to remain in communication

with Spirit, not just when I need help with a problem. I often connect with Spirit as I go along in my day, much like a baby elephant prefers to be in touch with her mother and the aunties of the herd.

Try to read only one section at a time — This is usually eight to twelve paragraphs and sometimes even that is too much for me. It took me about nine years to read the Course all the way through the first time. This is mainly because I had a busy life in those years. It is also due to the fact that when I took time to read, I went through it slowly, one section at a time. I remember one day I wanted to finish a chapter, so I read ten pages in a row. I told my best friend Kris, "I will never do that again!" My brain was overloaded. ACIM reading sessions are so much more effective when focusing on 'quality' versus 'quantity.'

This is not to say that you should take so many years to read the Course. I sometimes read more than one section in a day, but I do so in two separate sittings. Everyone reads at their own pace, as their schedule allows. My overall point is not to expect that you'll be able to read ACIM cover-to-cover in just a few weeks. The language and concepts have so much depth. It takes time to absorb the messages, because it is being understood at deeper levels than just our conscious mind.

FIP & COA versions— In this book I will use quotes from the 3rd Standard Edition from the Foundation for Inner Peace (FIP), published in 2007. There is another version that I use in my studies called *A Course in Miracles — Complete & Annotated Edition,* published by the Circle of Atonement (COA) in 2017. This Complete Edition (CE) is based on a new transcription of Helen's original handwritten notes by COA founder Robert

Perry. Some quotations from the CE will be included here and will be noted as such.

Getting started — With these considerations in mind, let's get started with this masterpiece by beginning at the beginning. It may be helpful to review a copy of either the FIP or COA books as we go over these components. If you don't have a copy of the book available, a free digital FIP version can be accessed at *acim.org*. Go to 'Read ACIM' and click on 'Entire ACIM Web Edition.' Alternatively, a digital edition of the COA's CE version can be downloaded from the Chrome browser by typing *acimce.app*.

Having a background in English, I use a mindful approach whenever I start reading a book. The first thing I do with any book is to check the copyright date because I want to consider the historical context of when it was published. Then I take time to review all of the preliminary materials. There are different introductory components in both books, which give background on the origins of each of these versions. Either book offers interesting preliminary information. You may also notice that the Table of Contents is quite intriguing. Reading the chapter and section titles reveals that the content of this book is indeed quite profound.

It's been said that the Course's wisdom teachings are holographic in the sense that, no matter which page you turn to, the healing messages feel relevant to your current situation. In addition, the whole message of the Course is sometimes presented in just one page. This is certainly the case as we arrive at the Introduction page. The content of the Introduction may not seem to make sense at first glance, but for those who are drawn to stay with the Course, the meaning is profoundly moving each time it is reviewed. I suggest reading through the Introduction to *A Course in Miracles*, but do not be concerned if there are some confusing lines. We will go over each line together.

INTRODUCTION

1.	This is a course in miracles. It is a required course. Only the time you take it is voluntary. Free will does not mean that you can establish the curriculum. It means only that you can elect what you want to take at a given time. The course does not aim at teaching the meaning of love, for that is beyond what can be taught. It does aim, however, at removing the blocks to the awareness of love's presence, which is your natural inheritance. The opposite of love is fear, but what is all-encompassing can have no opposite.

2.	This course can therefore be summed up very simply in this way:

Nothing real can be threatened.
Nothing unreal exists.
Herein lies the peace of God.

Now, you may have understood that perfectly, but chances are that it might have been a bit confusing. You might have resonated with certain lines, but perhaps you aren't quite sure about others. Let's go over each line grouping for further clarity.

Introduction Lines 1-5:

"This is a course in miracles."—This is a course, not The Course in Miracles. There are many paths back to Oneness, though this is a particularly effective one. [Note: Sometimes we refer to ACIM as 'the Course' for the sake of convenience, but it is still simply a course and not the only way to return our awareness to our True Home with God.]

"It is a required course."—The second line of the Introduction may be off-putting to new readers as it seems to imply that you are *required* to take this course. Rather, it is believed that this line was a response to Bill and Helen's determination to find a better way—and in that sense it was meant for the two of them. In the Manual for Teachers it is explained that this Course is just a special form of the "universal curriculum" of learning True Forgiveness [see ACIM M-1.4:1-10]. This line is simply stating that returning Home by learning True Forgiveness is everyone's destiny. There are many paths, but one destination: Oneness.

In addition, Helen Schucman was a professor of psychology, and the term "required course" was a part of her career lingo. We can see this in the next lines with related terms such as, "curriculum" and "elect."

"Only the time you take it is voluntary. Free will does not mean that you can establish the curriculum. It means only that you can elect what you want to take at a given time."— The first line, "Only the time you take it is voluntary," can cause confusion. As I understand it, this is saying "Because you have free will, you choose the point in time that you decide to take your learning pathway." Learning pathways are always available for us to choose to take them, and when we do, we finally access our healing potential.

In addition, our willingness to learn of our interconnected Oneness determines how quickly we complete the curriculum. We can take an accelerated course like ACIM, or a convoluted route that takes much longer, or something in-between. But we will not 'graduate' from the futile cycle of birth and death, until we learn our We-Are-One coursework here in classroom-Earth. We can procrastinate, deny and delay, but that just brings about more unpleasant experiences of separation. Eventually we will choose to be shown our way back Home to Oneness, which is our True Identity.

Introduction Lines 6-7:

"The course does not aim at teaching the meaning of love, for that is beyond what can be taught. It does aim, however, at removing the blocks to the awareness of love's presence, which is your natural inheritance." — There is a reason these blocks seem to exist: We began to believe that we were separate from God. ACIM explains that God's all-encompassing Love is ever-present, however when we thought we separated, we made barriers of guilt and fear in our mind. Like a wall of stones, these barriers block our awareness of God's ever-present Love, which is our natural state of mind.

Introduction Line 8:

"The opposite of love is fear, but what is all-encompassing can have no opposite." — It may be helpful to think of the first part of the line, "The opposite of love is fear," as a statement of what this dualistic world would have us believe.

It seems like the world is made of opposites — day and night, good and bad, love and fear. However, the nondualistic messages of the Course affirm that God's Love is all-encompassing. By definition, all-encompassing Love encompasses everything, everywhere, without opposites of any kind.

Introduction Lines 9-12:

"This Course can therefore be summed up very simply in this way:

Nothing real can be threatened.

Nothing unreal exists.

Herein lies the Peace of God."

Now, let's look at those amazing last four lines which encapsulate the entire Course beautifully. Upon first reading these lines, there may be a subtle recognition of Truth, even if you don't understand what they mean. They are just so resonant.

It might be helpful to think of the word 'real' in terms of 'eternal.' Nothing eternal can be threatened. If it is eternal and changeless, there is nothing which can affect changelessness. Anything that appears to be changeable is not eternal and cannot be real, therefore, it cannot actually exist.

Before delving into the discernment of eternal Truth from temporary illusion, it will be helpful to build some other foundations first. The take-home for now is that God's Love is eternal and all-encompassing; it is not possible for anything else to exist. Knowing this in our heart-of-hearts brings us the Peace of God. Even if you aren't sure why, at a deep level, you may already recognize these lines as a profound universal Truth.

Now that we have gone over some of the nuances in the Introduction, I invite you to read it through one more time.

INTRODUCTION

1.   This is a course in miracles. It is a required course. Only the time you take it is voluntary. Free will does not mean that you can establish the curriculum. It means only that you can elect what you want to take at a given time. The course does not aim at teaching the meaning of love, for that is beyond what can be taught. It does aim, however, at removing the blocks to the awareness of love's presence, which is your natural inheritance. The opposite of love is fear, but what is all-encompassing can have no opposite.

2.   This course can therefore be summed up very simply in this way:

Nothing real can be threatened.
Nothing unreal exists.
Herein lies the peace of God.

Do you feel a bit more comfortable with it? You may have noticed that the first time you read the Introduction, it might have seemed like gibberish. This can be the case with any section in the Course, especially in the first few chapters. For example, the first chapter lists fifty miracle principles and the first several times I read them, they went way over my head. Each time I review them now, they make more sense — though I still have to read them slowly and mindfully.

When you begin to read the Course, if you find the Text

difficult to understand, I recommend trying the Workbook Lessons. They flow much better, partly because Helen had been scribing the Course for years by the time she got to the Workbook Lessons so she was more acclimated to the process. Alternatively, some students begin by reading the Manual for Teachers, located near the back of the book. It simplifies the terms so when you read the Text, you have a sense of what it's talking about. My recommendation is to Ask Spirit, Pause & Listen for guidance on the most helpful approach for you. It may feel like you're making-up the ideas coming to you, but no worries, just go with them.

At first ACIM can be quite difficult to understand. With time and careful reading, the meaning emerges. I take a little time with it, focusing on the general meaning of each of the sentences. I don't try to analyze or extricate the whole meaning; I just read the sentence at hand and see what comes to me. If I feel reasonably comfortable that I have grasped what that particular sentence is saying, I move on to the next one.

Sometimes I don't feel like I fully understand, and I'm okay with that too. I table anything that doesn't make sense, and I just read on. A further explanation is often provided within the rest of the section. Even though there are aspects that make comprehension more challenging, and we will discuss those next, I feel it's best for new students not to try to figure out every single nuance of the Course. It will become much easier to understand with time and repetition. Like an Easter egg being immersed in a dye, the coloration is very faint at first. Then, each time it is immersed, the eggshell absorbs just a little more color, until it becomes saturated with a beautiful, vibrant hue.

CHAPTER 3

An Overview of Language Baggage

IN ORDER to study the Course, we read or listen to it in our language of choice. Words in any language can be extremely powerful, yet the limitations of our languages cannot fully express the depth of meaning that ACIM points to. In the Manual for Teachers, a section entitled 'What is the Role of Words in Healing?' explains:

> "Words can be helpful, particularly for the beginner, in helping concentration and facilitating the exclusion, or at least the control, of extraneous thoughts. Let us not forget, however, that words are but symbols of symbols. They are thus twice removed from reality." (ACIM: M-21.1:8-10)

And yet this is how we currently communicate. At this very moment, you are exploring abstract concepts by reading the words printed on this page. Though words cannot fully describe what exists beyond this world, we do the best we can with the tools at our disposal. So, when you begin to read ACIM, the first thing you may notice is that the language is not straightforward. Its complex sentence structures are elegantly poetic and, at first, this can be a bit overwhelming.

The following are examples of how ACIM's language style can cause confusion:

The "It" Factor—Often a subject is given in one sentence, then several more lines refer back to the subject using the pronoun "it." Sometimes the sentences would be too wordy to specify what each "it" refers to. However, when "it" is used multiple times in one or more paragraphs, it's easy to forget what "it" refers to. This can also occur with the use of "he," "this," "they," etc. When I get confused by recurrent pronouns, I take a moment to go back over the lines to find the subject. Here's an example:

> "The mind returns to <u>its</u> proper function only when <u>it</u> wills to know. This places <u>it</u> in the service of spirit, where perception is changed. The mind chooses to divide <u>itself</u> when <u>it</u> chooses to make <u>its</u> own levels. But <u>it</u> could not entirely separate <u>itself</u> from spirit, because <u>it</u> is from spirit that <u>it</u> derives <u>its</u> whole power to make or create." (ACIM: T-3.IV.5:6-9)

In this case, we can glance back through the lines to find that nearly all the "it" references are to "the mind." Sometimes it's a bit more challenging to figure out and if you can't at the time, no worries, just move on. There will be another explanation of the same idea somewhere in your reading that will make more sense.

The thing about "but"—ACIM sometimes uses "but" as an exclusionary descriptor, in the same way as "only."

- "It can be <u>but</u> my gratitude I earn." (ACIM: W-197)
- "The decision whether or not to listen to this course and follow it is <u>but</u> the choice between truth and

illusion." (ACIM: T-16.V.16:1)

If the use of the word 'but' causes confusion, it might be helpful to replace it in your mind with 'only.' For example, the previous line could be read as:

- "The decision whether or not to listen to this course and follow it is (only) the choice between truth and illusion."

I sometimes use the word 'simply.' This works in most cases, but not all of them:

- "The decision whether or not to listen to this course and follow it is (simply) the choice between truth and illusion."

The use of the word 'but' in this way may seem archaic, however, after a while, it isn't as bothersome.

Double Negatives—Another potential problem for comprehension involves the use of double and even triple negatives. Sometimes the nuance of the sentence really calls for a double negative, but other times it can cause confusion.

- "You do <u>not</u> have to continue to believe what is <u>not</u> true unless you choose to do so." (ACIM: T-2.I.3:3)
- "You have allowed the Thought of your reality to enter your mind, and because you invited it, it will abide with you. Your love for it will <u>not</u> allow you to betray yourself, and you could <u>not</u> enter into a relationship where it could <u>not</u> go with you, for you would <u>not</u> want to be apart from it." (ACIM: T-16. VI.9:3-4)

Between the "it's," "but's" and "not's," it might take time to glean the meaning—but it will be time well-spent! Just like reading

Shakespearean verse, it gets easier as you become accustomed to the style of the language.

Masculine Pronouns—Another potential concern is the use of masculine pronouns which has caused some people to drop ACIM like a hot potato. The Foundation for Inner Peace has gotten considerable pushback on this subject. Their position is that using the neutral pronoun "it" to describe God and the Holy Spirit just doesn't work. I agree in principle, but I find that "He" is only slightly better than "It." Fortunately, we now are developing alternative descriptors that don't require assigning a dualistic gender to a Nonbinary, Limitless Being.

Biblical Terminology—This is a multi-layered subject and describing the nuances is not a simple task, so this is just an overview. As I understand it, the reason for using biblical terminology in the Course is to help people understand Christian-based concepts from the Bible that have either been misinterpreted or entirely misappropriated. The main point is that the Course clarifies the meaning of biblical terms to consistently convey God's all-encompassing Love. Unfortunately, even though the traditional concepts are revitalized to convey God's Love, people can still be triggered by ACIM's religious terminology. They shut down quickly when they read biblical terms in the Course because their associations with the *old* connotations bring up previous religious inculcation, or even traumatic experiences.

I can certainly understand their struggle with religious triggers. I often could not handle my own language baggage, and I was very close to walking away. When I began reading the Course, I held a deep-seated grudge against God because I refused to accept the wrathful God of the Bible punishing His own creations. I couldn't even look at the word 'God' without a hostile reaction. For the first year of reading ACIM, I actually wrote over the word God, penning in the word 'Good.'

Also, until I understood the reasoning for the use of the word 'sin,' I scratched it out as I gritted my teeth with righteous indignation and wrote in 'error.' I didn't understand that *we* believe we sinned when we tried to separate from God; but God is only all-encompassing Love, so in the ultimate reality, sin is impossible. The only reason ACIM uses the word 'sin' is to explain our own perspective, because we believe we did something unforgivable.

- "Sin is insanity. It is the means by which the mind is driven mad, and seeks to let illusions take the place of truth." (ACIM: W-pII.4.1:1-2)
- "Sin is the home of all illusions, which but stand for things imagined, issuing from thoughts that are untrue." (ACIM: W-pII.4.3:1)
- "There is no sin." (ACIM: W-pII.4.5:5)

Sin is impossible because we continue to be an absolutely integral part of God's all-encompassing Love.

Other religious terms that can carry emotionally charged connotations include: God's Will, judgment, salvation, justice, the Kingdom of Heaven, Son of God, and several more. Yet *A Course in Miracles* thoroughly explains each one in terms of God's all-encompassing Love.

One of the most important examples of a potentially charged biblical term is 'the Atonement.' ACIM uses this concept in a completely different way than how we typically think of it. According to traditional interpretations of the Bible, it is believed that all of humanity has sinned against God. In order to avoid eternal damnation, this wrathful God demanded retribution for our transgressions. Consequently, Jesus had to be crucified so the innocent blood of the sacrificial lamb 'atoned' for all our sins.

[Note: Something unexpected happened while I was writing about the traditional religious interpretation of the Atonement. I began experiencing deep-seated triggers about this disturbing description. In ACIM, the Atonement means the complete healing of the mind that thought it was separate from God. It is achieved through True Forgiveness, because this method removes the blocks to our awareness of God's all-encompassing Love. In contrast, the old connotation of the Atonement feels overwhelmingly wrong. I was so intensely triggered by the idea that God demands retribution for all of mankind's sins that it was making me dizzy. As tension gripped my abdomen and throat, a huge wave of resentment flooded my mind like a tsunami. I did not even realize this intense anger was there until it surfaced quite unexpectedly. This lets me know me that I have True Forgiveness work to do. Though my feelings are extremely disharmonious as I write this, this is a good thing because it is alerting me to an unconscious block that has been keeping my mind unhealed.

This may seem odd to mention here, but it is actually extremely important to notice and pay attention to. What students of *A Course in Miracles* do when we are triggered is to allow our feelings and beliefs to come into our awareness. We Ask Spirit, Pause & Listen as we look at those feelings and beliefs. If we suppress our feelings and pretend that we aren't bothered by a situation, we are *blocking* the healing with a 'spiritual bypass' which keeps the grievance locked in our mind. I use a step-by-step process of looking at the situation with Spirit to Truly Forgive it. We will circle back to the True Forgiveness Steps later in the book, after we go over the foundational concepts.]

In contrast to the biblical concept of the Atonement, ACIM's Atonement is the recognition that, though we thought we were separate from God, this cannot be True. Then we Ask Spirit to dispel our layered beliefs in separation. I think of it as a process of reconciliation and reunion. Here is ACIM's basic explanation of the Atonement:

- "Atonement means correction, or the undoing of errors." (ACIM: M-18.4:6)
- "Miracles are part of an interlocking chain of forgiveness which, when completed, is the Atonement." (ACIM: T-1.I.25:1)
- "Our emphasis is now on healing. The miracle is the means, the Atonement is the principle, and healing is the result." (ACIM: T-2.IV.1:1-2)

Any ACIM term or concept that triggers resentment is actually providing a valuable opportunity to release a block that does not serve us. I suggest Asking Spirit, "This is how I feel about it right now, and I don't like it! Please help me see this differently." Then Pause & Listen for a message, vision or a sense of Peace to emerge.

Ken Wapnick, the first teacher of the Course, expressed that there is actually a potential benefit to struggling with the language of the Course. He explains that as the language challenges engage the ego, the messages are permeating our mind at deeper levels. So if you read it and say, "I don't like what this says. I completely disagree with it." Or, "I have no idea what this means. It's way over my head. I can't figure it out." Don't be discouraged, there is much more going on under the surface that we are not consciously aware of. I encourage you to simply keep reading a little bit every day, Asking Spirit, Pausing & Listening as needed. I also encourage ACIM students with religious triggers to try using companion books and study groups to continue with the Course long enough to appreciate the Course's revitalized use of these terms.

With these considerations in mind, if a student is still struggling with language barriers, there is another option available. In 2010, Elizabeth Cronkhite published *The Message of A Course in Miracles: A Translation of the Text in Plain Language*. It provides gender-neutral descriptors and fewer religiously charged terms. This translation also uses more understandable vocabulary and sentence structures while preserving the Course's nondualistic messages. It might be helpful for people who are highly averse to the use of masculine pronouns and religious language or the complexity of the Course. One potential downside with this plain language version is that it is rather plain. The messages have been preserved, but the writing is not as beautiful or engaging.

Since I started studying the Course in 2008, and the Plain Language version was published in 2010, I had already made huge strides with most of my language baggage by the time I found it. I did take a look at it, and I meant to study it further, but I ended up continuing to use the FIP edition. I am pleased that the Plain Language version is available, though. For those who are truly overwhelmed with language baggage, this could be a wonderful option worth exploring.

The overall message for the language style of *A Course in Miracles* is to try not to let the verbiage trip you up. After reading for many months or years, it's much easier to follow. Much like reading Shakespeare, it gets easier with time, and then you gain a deep appreciation for the artistry of the language.

CHAPTER 4

FYI's for Introducing ACIM Concepts

THE PREVIOUS chapter illustrates how the Course's langu-age can be confusing or off-putting. Yet there is another aspect that can be even more challenging—certain ACIM concepts are abstract and hard to understand. The Course describes a completely different conceptualization of the world than what we are accustomed to. Explaining this different approach is not easy because we are learning about it from our current limited perspective.

This reminds me of how difficult it can be for people who have had a near-death experience to fully explain what occurred while they crossed over into the between-life realm and then returned to their current body. The International Association of Near Death Studies has done extensive research in this field (see *iands.org*). To get a sense of this language limitation, interviews with NDExperiencers are available on social media platforms.

NDE's are often extremely expansive and life-changing and many NDExperiencers feel stifled by our limited language when trying to put the abstract experience into words. Even though they do their best to explain it, the experience reaches far beyond our limited viewpoint. In addition, what people experience across the veil may contradict many of our belief systems. Fixed religious beliefs, scientific beliefs and self-limiting physical senses can interfere with our comprehension as we try to listen and learn. We tend to think we know what is and isn't possible, but from our limited viewpoint, we simply cannot understand the bigger picture.

Likewise, in regard to the Course, our limited language cannot fully encapsulate its profound concepts. Additionally, our preconceived ideas, religious, scientific, or otherwise, can cause resistance to the wider viewpoint. Even if you are confused by ACIM's concepts, I encourage you not to give up, just know it takes willingness, an open mind and time to understand the ideas being expressed. Your efforts will be extremely worthwhile.

Honestly, the concepts outlined in the Course make more sense than anything I have ever studied in my life! They offer reliable means for creating great change in our lives. This is one reason why I felt guided to write this book, to help familiarize new and returning students with the basic concepts. Then when you come across them in the Course, you will already have a framework in mind, because if you don't understand why the Course is saying what it says, it can be quite confusing.

To that end, I offer some suggestions here for approaching the study of *A Course in Miracles*. First, Ask Spirit to facilitate an understanding that supersedes language and the thinking mind. 'Ask Spirit, Pause & Listen' is a phrase I use frequently because, as this ACIM quote describes, we have unseen support available at all times.

"(God's) Voice speaks for Him in all situations and

in every aspect of all situations, telling you exactly what to do to call upon His strength and His protection." (ACIM: W-47.3:2)

It may take practice to attune yourself to the help that is available, but you will soon begin to feel the effects of Asking, Pausing & Listening for help.

My next suggestion is, 'Give it time.' There are many other learning pathways, but the Course is so efficient, effective and helpful. In other words, I can think of no better way to spend my time!

When I talk about giving it time, there are a couple meanings to this suggestion. First, it means making time to study the text and/or practice the lessons every day, or at least regularly. Taking time to read the daily lessons is especially helpful. After a while, you may gradually feel less inclined to spend time focusing on the news or getting into controversies on social media. You may prefer to spend your time enjoying family and friends, crafting, journaling, or snuggling with your furry friends. You may start to feel more peaceful and less conflicted just by taking a little time to study the Course each day.

'Give it time' can also mean that you may find yourself studying the Course as a life-long practice. You may not start out that way, you may expect to read it and then move on to the next spiritual teaching. However, I found that once I started feeling the benefits of the Course, I wanted to continue spending time with it.

It's funny how students become more and more interested. We're loving the ideas, we're resonating all over the place, and then we look up and realize it's been five years since we opened the book for the first time. By that point, we want to continue studying. There is a draw, an attraction, a recognition of universal wisdom within us, that keeps us connected to the Course.

I think of ACIM as my oxygen-line connecting me to an old-fashioned diving bell as I traverse the rocky underwater terrain of this alien world that is not my True Home. I hear so many people say they feel alien here, they don't fit in, they struggle to be at peace, they know the set-up of the world feels very off. The conditionality, the uncertainty, the disparities are very not-right feeling, but people believe they have no choice so they feel obligated to endure. If you have felt this too, you just might find ACIM concepts quite helpful. A bit mind blowing, but helpful, indeed!

Students can have trouble grasping ACIM's nondualistic concepts because dualistic thought patterns have influenced us since birth, and even for many eons before that. The old patterns don't work very well, but they influence our mental picture of the way the world works. For example, we sometimes hear that God created this world in order for life to experience itself. The theory goes that this world provides God with a playground with which to learn and grow through dualistic experiences. But this begs the question, "If God is Perfect Love, how would God benefit from experiencing pain and fear? How could misery improve Perfect Love?" Because God is Perfect Oneness, God doesn't need any type of dualistic experiences to become more Perfect, and neither do we.

We have been told that we need to experience dark to understand Light, sadness to appreciate Joy, and fear to know to Love. ACIM explains that Light, Joy and Love are our natural characteristics. We are already the perfect, innocent, beloved Child of God, and we do not need darkness, misery or fear to expand our knowledge. Dualistic experiences are not fun. Duality dictates that if there is a winner, there must be a loser, leading to a competitive "kill-or-be-killed" mentality. Why would Perfect Love want to kill in order to survive? Why would God's all-encompassing Love only be given to some people, but exclude others? That does not make sense.

We know these stuck thought patterns don't work, but we try to go along with it, since we seem to have no choice. ACIM offers us a choice, and it is not nearly as difficult as trying to manage these incongruities. It takes practice to not get carried away on an emotional roller coaster. And if we do spiral, we step back as soon as we remember that we do have a choice in how we react to people and events in this world. Any time we feel an upset or a grievance coming up, we do not suppress it, we recognize it as a cue to apply True Forgiveness. We Ask Spirit, Pause & Listen for help to dispel what doesn't feel right. If you'd like to, you can try that right now.

First, slowly take in a full breath, gently let it out, and repeat a few times. When you feel centered, Ask Spirit to help you with the application of True Forgiveness. Let a recent upset or grievance come to mind—I like to write notes about whatever is coming up. It can be a memory, a current issue, or a worry. Now tune-in to the off-feeling associated with it. Pay attention to the feelings that are coming up, allow the emotions to be felt rather than avoided. Next, note the beliefs you have around this issue. It might be surprising what comes up, so just keep exploring the feelings and beliefs as they unfold in your mind.

Next, Ask Spirit "Spirit, I feel worried or guilty about
_____." Or "I am holding a grievance against someone. I don't
like feeling this way, please help me see this differently." Nice
easy breaths as you Pause & Listen for a bit. A new way of
thinking about it might emerge. An image may come to mind
or you may feel more peaceful about the situation. It could shift
in that moment or sometime later, but at some point, you may
notice that you do not feel the same way about the issue.

Sometimes you will feel a physical sensation that occurs
simultaneously as your mind experiences the paradigm shift.
It may be the sensation of chill-bumps, or the sunlight gets
brighter at the very instant that you have a realization. Maybe
a related song 'randomly' plays in the background. You might
hear a bell at the same moment you have an idea, synchronis-
tically confirming that insight. I've experienced all of these,
and many others. I put those experiences in the category of
miracles, because they indicate a dawning awareness, a release of a mindset that did not serve me.

If you don't notice these, not to worry, each person has their
very own synchronous clues, and sometimes they can be quite
subtle. Also, sometimes people block the process because it
makes them fearful, or they deny the sign because they are
doubtful that it could happen to them. Just give yourself per-
mission to allow it to unfold naturally, relax, and give it time.

If you do notice something that feels resonant, receive
whatever it is with gratitude—acknowledge the shift. Try not
to over-analyze it, simply take a moment to pause and breathe
it in to really receive it. It's best not to force these resonances,
but don't block them, just allow them to flow. And then, go
with the flow! I also like to check-in a day later to see if I feel

the same way. Often the feelings have been transformed by then and I feel released from the upset that was burdening my mind.

As stated before, the incongruous ways of the world are imposed upon us from infancy onward and from this lifetime to the next. We carry with us a whole bunch of preconceived notions about what is going on in our lives here on Earth. There are some concepts within the Course that seem to directly contradict the dogmatic beliefs of certain traditional religions. That can feel uncomfortable—so what do we do if that happens? Ask Spirit, Pause & Listen? Yes, exactly!

For instance, the Course has a different explanation for the origin of the world than what is depicted in the Bible. Understanding this might be difficult for people coming from a conventional religious upbringing. However, when I first began reading ACIM's explanation for why and how the world came to be, I was thrilled. That's because I'd never been able to accept that a Loving Creator would subject us to wrath, punishment, struggle and strife. This is what we've been told by the Bible and traditional religions, but it never made sense to me. I searched for years to understand and nothing gave me a satisfying answer until I read *The Disappearance of the Universe* and then *A Course in Miracles*. Once I got over my language baggage, I have never, ever looked back!

The 1998 movie *The Truman Show* comes to mind when thinking about the incongruent nature of our world. The main character Truman doesn't know that every day of his life is being live-streamed as a reality show that has been viewed by millions of people since the day he was born. He believes he is living a normal life until he begins to notice little inconsistencies that started with a production light fixture falling out of the sky onto the ground. As he begins to pay more attention, he uncovers more oddities in his world that he cannot reconcile. After realizing he's living in a completely artificial world, he seeks to leave the set. When he finally finds the exit, he follows his path to freedom.

In a way, we have all been living *The Truman Show* as we try to navigate this dysfunctional world. We struggle to make it work, but it never does work, and then we finally say, "There must be a better way." As a better way unfolds, it can be unsettling to deconstruct what we've been told all our lives. Yet the alternative is to pretend that the chaos of duality is acceptable.

It may feel disconcerting let go of old paradigms, because we want to hold onto something we're familiar with, so we don't feel like we're free-falling. Feeling unsettled as we expand our awareness means that we're getting close to a paradigm shift. Asking Spirit, Pausing & Listening can help as we explore new conceptualizations of the world. Being willing to simply consider the possibilities is quite helpful indeed.

CHAPTER 5

The Most Basic ACIM Concept— Our Belief in Separation from God

Now that we have covered the background information on *A Course in Miracles*, we'll look into the key ACIM concepts that helped me find the answer to my question, "WHY is there so much suffering in this world, and WHY am I living here?" For each of the steps I attempt to explain, questions will inevitably arise, many of which will be answered as our exploration progresses. It is not necessary to fully grasp or believe them, instead just let them marinate for a while. Feel what they may mean to you, rather than trying to intellectualize them.

As we embark on this explanation of WHY, it's good to Ask Spirit to help with this learning process. If you are willing, take a moment to center and connect with Spirit. Ask Spirit for help to understand these insights, then Pause & Listen as you slowly breathe in and out for 20-30 seconds. Receive any encouraging thought, image or sense of peace that may come —it is for you from Spirit.

Now to begin the description of ACIM's most basic concept: Our mistaken belief in separation from God. You have probably heard at some point in your life that this world is an illusion. That can feel threatening and it doesn't sit well with the inhabitants of planet Earth…unless you suspected it all along because everything feels so incongruent. For those inhabitants of Earth who haven't yet sensed that the world is an illusion, it's a very understandable misunderstanding. For just a smidge of background on this insight, let's look at perspectives from world religions, quantum scientists, writers, poets, and the songs of rock stars.

Worldwide Religions teach the illusory nature of the world

- Throughout Buddhist wisdom teachings, the world is described as an illusion. For example, in the Diamond Sutra the Buddha said, "All conditioned phenomena are like a dream, an illusion, a bubble, a shadow, like dew or a flash of lightning." Everything in the world is impermanent and will come to an end at some point in time.

- The Jewish teachings of the Kabbalah include many references to the world as illusion. Chapter 1.1, called The Great Illusion, says the most fundamental principle of Judaism is "that everything we see is only a figment of our imagination."

- From the Chandayoga Upanishad, found within the Hindu Vedic text, "You could have a golden treasure buried beneath your feet, and walk over it again and again, yet never find it because you don't realize it is there. Just so, all beings live every moment in the city of the Divine, but never find the Divine because it is hidden by the well of illusion."

Quantum scientists are discovering the illusory nature of the world

- "If quantum mechanics has not profoundly shocked you, you haven't understood it yet. Everything we call real cannot be regarded as real." — Niels Bohr, quantum physicist

- "The illusion that we are separate from each other is an optical delusion of consciousness." — Albert Einstein, theoretical physicist

- "Vedanta teaches us that consciousness is singular, all happenings are played out in one universal consciousness and there is no multiplicity of selves." — Erwin Schrödinger, quantum physicist (the cat dude)

- "In the long run, it is far more dangerous to adhere to illusion than to face what the actual fact is." — David Bohm, theoretical physicist

Writers, poets and philosophers are observing that the world is an illusory dream

- "Quantum physics is now proving what the ancients long knew. Time, distance and matter are all illusions. Everything is interconnected. We are one." — Bronwell Landrum, author and entrepreneur

- "If you can recognize illusion as illusion, it dissolves. The recognition of illusion is also its ending. Its survival depends on your mistaking it for reality." — Eckhart Tolle, author and spiritual teacher

- "Is not this world an illusion? And yet it fools everybody." — Angela Carter, writer, poet and journalist

- "We are all such stuff as dreams are made on, and our little life is rounded with a sleep." — William Shakespeare, playwright and poet

- "The world is all a fleeting show, for man's illusion given the smiles of joy, the tears of woe, deceitful shine, deceitful flow, there's nothing true but Heaven." — Charles Lamb, essayist and poet

The songs of rock stars allude to the world as just a fantasy

- "…The fog of illusion, the fog of confusion is hanging all over the world…" —Van Morrison, Aryan Mist

- "Is this the real life, or is this just fantasy; caught in a landslide, no escape from reality? Open your eyes, look up to the skies and see…" — Queen, Bohemian Rhapsody

- "… Don't be fooled by the radio, the TV or the magazines, they show you photographs of how your life should be, but they're just someone else's fantasy. So if you think your life is complete confusion, because you never win the game, just remember that it's a Grand illusion, 'cause deep inside we're all the same. We're all the same..." — Styx, The Grand Illusion

So, what is all this about the world being an illusion? And if it is an illusion, WHY do we seem to be in it? That is the WHY so many are seeking and searching to find out! Fortunately, *A Course in Miracles* provides a comprehensive response to these questions. Chapter 27 of ACIM's Text contains a concise little wisdom nugget that, for me, is the Holy Grail of WHY. It may not be very understandable the first time through, but we'll go over it in detail:

> "Into eternity, where all is one, there crept a tiny, mad idea, at which the Son of God remembered not to laugh. In his forgetting did the thought become a serious idea, and possible of both accomplishment and real effects. Together, we can laugh them both away, and understand that time cannot intrude upon eternity. It is a joke to think that time can come to circumvent eternity, which means there is no time."
> (ACIM: T-27.VIII.6:2-5)

This can be difficult to wrap our minds around, so don't be discouraged if this is confusing. We'll go over each line together.

"Into eternity, where all is One" — It is important to realize that our eternal Essence, IS One and remains One. 'Eternity' is God together with All of us, United-as-One, eternally interconnected by all-encompassing, Perfect Love.

"There crept a tiny, mad idea at which the Son of God remembered not to laugh." — First, I want to clarify two linguistic aspects of this line that can be confusing. It's helpful to understand that 'mad' in this context means 'mad-crazy' not 'mad-angry.' The reason the tiny, mad idea is insane is that within the One Mind, it is impossible to exist anywhere that God is not.

Another potentially confusing phrase is found at the end of the line, 'remembered not to laugh.' It could sound like it is saying, 'we remembered that we weren't supposed to laugh.' However, the emphasis should be on both words 'remembered-not,' in the same way we say 'forget-me-not.' The meaning is 'the Son of God forgot to laugh' at the tiny, insane idea of separation.

Now to put it all together, in a small part of the One Mind, the 'tiny, mad idea' started as an innocent daydream. The idea that was dreamed-up was a very simple thought: "Hmm, I wonder what it would be like if I went over here by myself, apart from God, for a little bit." The tiny, mad idea was so insignificant, it was meaningless when we first had the thought — but then we forgot to laugh at the absurdity of the idea of going off alone.

"In his forgetting did the thought become a serious idea"—Here is where the knowledge of our Perfect Oneness was shattered, becoming a false belief in twoness. We took the idea so seriously that it seemed to become the truth.

"And possible in both accomplishment and real effects." —Because our mind has the capacity to create anything we want to see, we mistakenly misused our immense powers to generate an experience of separation from God. Then, because we immediately began experiencing the effects of separation, we believed we actually did accomplish it.

A Jewish saying describes hell as distance from God. This accounts for the sense of separation we perceive as we experience living on Earth. Our seeming separation from God feels like hell, and the further we pull away from God, the more hellish our perceptions become.

"Together, we can laugh them both away, and understand that time cannot intrude upon eternity." —With help from Spirit, we can laugh away the cause and the effects of our mistaken belief in separation. Whew, this is good news! Once we understand that the little bubble of separation we thought we made cannot be real, time is no longer needed. Then we will return our awareness back to our True Home of Perfect Oneness. The key word for the process of shifting back to our True Home is 'Together.' It cannot be done alone, my friends — Together Is Home.

"It is a joke to think that time can come to circumvent eternity, which means there is no time." —Aha! Here is the grand-finale statement, wrapping-up all those that went before. We forgot to laugh at our innocent joke of thinking we could be separate from God, which is impossible. We thought we separated, but we were mistaken. It was all an error, nothing more. And this is WHY the world we seem to experience is merely an illusion, which is exactly what science and many wisdom teachings have told us over and over. There is no time, no space, no world—there is no space-time bubble. There is only Eternity, which is an endless experience of Perfect Love.

In summary, we had an innocent thought of separation, but then we believed it. We misused our creative powers to 'make' a multiverse that acts out trillions of scenarios of separation. We have gotten lost in the labyrinth of the mind that believes we separated—really, really lost. We cannot find our way out of the little bubble of space-time that we made in a part of our mind—our 'thought experiment' gone wrong.

A gravity-pocket our thoughts fell into, where a part of our mind went upside down, inside-out, and backwards. And we know this. We sense it. We feel it. At our very core, we know this world is very, very wrong, and now we can conceptualize WHY!

Here's a simple metaphor for our tiny, mad idea of separation gone viral. Someone says, "Hey, don't think of a purple elephant".... And what just happened? Very likely, you thought of a purple elephant. Similarly, the false idea of separation got into our awareness and we kept reinforcing it, rather than dismissing it. Just like that purple elephant we don't want to picture in our mind, it keeps recurring, and getting bigger and more prominent in our mind.

My own acronym for describing this imaginary experience is the Old Original Perceived Separation (the OOPS). It's 'Old' because it occurred eons ago at the beginning of space-time. It's 'Original' because the original tiny, mad idea of separation is the origin of our misperceptions. It's 'Perceived' because our mind generates experiences that we *perceive* to be real, but they are false perceptions. It's 'Separation' because we believe we are separate from God, but this is impossible, so it is simply an 'OOPS.'

The Holy Spirit, the Voice for God, continuously Calls us, wanting to help our separated mind return to its True Home. However, because of free will, Spirit cannot just shake us awake and whisk us back to our Oneness. We chose to believe we were separate, and we must be willing to Ask for, and accept, help to choose again. Help is always available, and it is further enabled when we Ask for help. This is why our Homecoming MUST be Together with Spirit and with each other. We are lost, Spirit knows the way Home, but we must be willing to join together and follow Spirit Home.

Discovering this provided the answer to the WHY that I had been seeking all my life, and I remember the very day it coalesced in my awareness. It was on January 22, 2008, as I was reading *The Disappearance of the Universe*. The insights were unfolding with each sentence in the book. As a dawning awareness of the WHY swept over me, I got up and looked at my reflection in the mirror. In that moment of breathtaking insight, I finally began to understand the miserable scenarios of separation we seem to see in the world. Time stood still for a long moment as an overwhelming, expansive feeling welled-up from my heart-space—a miracle. This expanded sensation was exhilarating. Finally, the WHY was being comprehensively explained!

My heart still sings a song of gratitude for this great epiphany: "Thank you, Spirit, thank you, so much!" Now, I want to help those who seek these same answers to understand the problem so we can use our power of decision to choose again. This time, we are deciding for Spirit, which is exactly what the Course helps us do.

CHAPTER 6

Preparing for the Explanation of the OOPS

THE previous chapter describes the most basic ACIM concept—that we seem to be here because we had an innocent thought of separation from Oneness that went viral. More details in the following chapters will help make the situation even more understandable. However, before describing the step-by-step progression of what seemed to happen, I've got a little housekeeping to do. This chapter includes a few topics for consideration before we continue with the step-by-step progression of the OOPS.

To avoid level confusion, be practical — Now that we've discussed the illusory nature of this false simulation called the multiverse, it might be tempting to either quit doing anything at all; or to behave brashly because, "Heck-fire, the world isn't real—Let's go crazy!" Well, let's sit with this for a bit instead.

Some good advice given in DU, and in other Course-related books, is to 'be practical.' [Note: Some Course teachers say, 'Be normal.' And that can make sense, however, 'normal' behavior on this planet is almost exclusively dualistic, which reinforces the illusion.] As a student of the Course, we know that everyone and everything is an interconnected part of

Oneness. Yet, it certainly does not appear so in the world. Consequently, while we learn to apply this wisdom with perfect consistency, it is best to 'be practical' while navigating this realm. It is a process of learning to be an observer, to 'be in the world, not of the world,' while we learn to release our fears to the Holy Spirit.

> "Your task is not to seek for love, but merely to seek
> and find all of the barriers within yourself that you
> have built against it." (ACIM: T-16.IV.6:1)

The part of the mind that believes it's separate has entangled itself into an intricate web of incorrect beliefs. We now understand that the cause is in the mind, but there are many layers of defenses that don't just evaporate once we realize the world is not what we thought it was. Like being stuck in a crevasse with debris from a rockslide entrapping us, there is a delicate process of extrication. The Holy Spirit has a plan to help us, but the process must be gradual and gentle. This is why the study of the Course may be a life-long journey. Each day, as we are willing to receive help, the Holy Spirit is able to remove a few layers of debris from our mind that have been blocking our awareness of Love's eternal presence. Gradually the Truth shines through the defenses of our mind.

> "Each small step will clear a little of the darkness away,
> and understanding will finally come to lighten every
> corner of the mind that has been cleared of the de-
> bris that darkens it." (ACIM: W-9.2:5)

So, while the removal of the barriers of guilt and fear takes place at the level of the mind, we still have practical needs at the level of form.

"The body is merely part of your experience in the physical world…. However, it is almost impossible to deny its existence in this world. Those who do so are engaging in a particularly unworthy form of denial." (ACIM: T-2.IV.3:8-11)

[Note: The term 'unworthy' has a not-so-great connotation, but the rest of the section explains the meaning more appropriately. For now, it's fine to use the term 'unhelpful' instead.] In order to avoid level confusion, while we believe we are a body in this world, it is best to be practical by simply doing the things that need to be done. Take care of the body in a reasonable way, take walks, work, eat, and do the daily tasks that are asked of us. I think of this in terms of the Buddhist practice of living the Middle Way—not too extreme either way, not too austere, yet also not too body-identified with worldly possessions and accomplishments. Simply be as mindfully present as possible, while remaining willing to learn how to return our separated mind to Perfect Oneness.

As we continue to do the work of healing our mind, we might react less strongly to upsets in the world. [Note: the Light coming through the window got a lot brighter when I wrote that. I pay attention to those cues, knowing that shifts are occurring.] Many students have noticed that their reactions to outward events would have been much more dramatic if they had not been studying the Course. That has certainly been the case for me.

While living in a practical way, we don't focus on fixing the effects in the world. We focus on healing the cause in the mind, which is based on True Forgiveness of our false beliefs that are keeping us stuck in old patterns. After following our

True Forgiveness practice, if we are drawn to do something in the external world, we follow our inner guidance. So, if you decide to study the Course, the take-home for this caveat is: While working on True Forgiveness at the level of the mind, be practical at the level of form.

The belief that Heaven must be boring — The next topic for consideration is the reaction people tend to have about the prospect of returning to Heaven. Sometimes people assume that Heaven, being eternally changeless, must be pretty boring. From our ego-based perspective within the space-time bubble, that seems plausible. Yet, as this excerpt from *The Disappearance of the Universe* explains, Heaven is not even remotely boring. This misconception is clarified at the very beginning of the book when Gary has just met his teaching companions, Pursah and Arten.

> PURSAH: The only true reality is God or pure spirit, which in Heaven are synonymous, and God and pure spirit have no form. Thus there is no concept of male or female in Heaven…

After some discussion, Gary returns to the comment about pure spirit being formless and genderless.

> GARY: That's cool, but I don't know if I like this idea of no male and female in Heaven.
> PURSAH: There are no differences in Heaven and no changes. Everything is constant. That's the only way it can be completely dependable instead of chaotic.

GARY: Isn't that kind of boring?

PURSAH: Let me ask you something, Gary. Is sex boring?

GARY: Not in my book.

PURSAH: Well, imagine the very peak of a perfect sexual orgasm, except this orgasm never stops. It keeps going on forever with no decrease in its powerful and flawless intensity.

GARY: You have my attention.

PURSAH: The physical act of sex doesn't even come close to the incredible bliss of Heaven. It's just a poor, made-up imitation of union with God. It's a false idol to fix your attention on the body and the world with just enough of a payoff to keep you coming back for more. It's very similar to a narcotic. Heaven, on the other hand, is a perfect, indescribable ecstasy that never ceases.

Isn't that good to know? The ego makes it sound like reconciling and reuniting together as One is a bad idea, urging us not to let our 'independent' spirit lose its autonomy. However, the belief that Heaven is boring is actually an ego-based ploy to block our decision to return to Love. We have no idea of the endless blissful ecstasy our separated mind is missing out on.

Looking at the steps of the OOPS—There are several places in the Course that say it is not helpful to over-analyze the Old Original Perceived Separation. For example, Line 5 in the Introduction of the Clarification of Terms says:

> "To study the error itself does not lead to correction,
> if you are indeed to succeed in overlooking the er-
> ror." (ACIM: C-in.1:5)

"The error" was the 'tiny, mad idea' of separation that we forgot to laugh at. These lines in the Clarification of Terms advise
us to avoid over-analyzing the error because that, in itself, will
not help us get past the error. If we keep emphasizing the error, rather than the correction (which is the True Forgiveness
process), we reinforce the problem and block the solution.

It might seem a little ironic that the next part of this book
will be exploring exactly what those lines are referencing, the
steps of the original error. To me, what the Course is saying
here, is it does not serve us to dwell on the OOPS—we don't
want to beat ourselves up about it. Instead, as we learn how
the error was made, we can forgive ourselves and release it.

> "Time really, then, goes backward to an instant so
> ancient that it is beyond all memory, and past even
> the possibility of remembering. Yet because it is an
> instant that is relived again and again and still again,
> it seems to be now." (ACIM: M-2.4:1-2)

Here's a top tip about forgiving the OOPS: We do not have
to go back to the original error to forgive it. Whatever comes
up in our *current* sphere of awareness is a symbolic repeating pattern from the OOPS. As we feel our emotions being triggered now, we are ready to look at the ego's tactics
symbolically repeating the OOPS. Once we recognize the
unhealthy pattern, we can Ask Spirit to help us step out of
the pattern because we have changed our minds about its
helpfulness to us.

This is key to understanding the Course, but when I was

new to the Course, I couldn't comprehend what I needed to do differently until I could grasp the nature of the original problem. All of the steps of the OOPS are described in the Course, however, not in a step-by-step progression. For me, learning the concepts from different parts of the Course was pretty hit and miss, which was confusing, making it a struggle to figure them out. This can be an overwhelming problem, as evidenced by the number of students who give up trying to study the Course.

As an educator, when I am instructing a class, I begin by presenting the foundational information in an organized and understandable format. For example, in an English class, the basic rules of grammar should first be explained with a structured and consistent progression of concepts. Then when students are given an assignment, they will be able to apply those concepts as they do their homework. If they don't understand the foundational principles of grammar, how can they complete their assignments?

The Course teaches us that Earth is our classroom, True Forgiveness is our learning objective, and events in our lives are our homework assignments. In my opinion, outlining the Course's explanation of how we ended up in the space-time bubble makes getting out of that bubble much more achievable. This is especially important because the Course says that we've been symbolically repeating the same mistake ever since time began.

> "Each day, and every minute in each day, and every instant that each minute holds, you but relive the single instant when the time of terror took the place of love." (ACIM: T-26.V.13:1)

When I'm instructing a class, if students are making the same errors over and over again, it's helpful to assess what is interfering with the student's comprehension. This entails making sure students understand the fundamental concepts so they can complete their assignments correctly. It is also helpful to review their homework assignments to understand where the errors are being made. As the instruction is adjusted accordingly, the likelihood of success with future assignments is exponentially improved.

Likewise, I feel it is helpful for students of *A Course in Miracles* to understand the fundamental steps of the perceived separation within the space-time bubble. We've been repeating the same mistakes over and over again, because most of us do not understand why we seem to be on Earth, or how to undo our perceived entrapment. This is why the following chapters explain the basic step-by-step progression of how the separation seemed to play out. After the OOPS is described, the steps for True Forgiveness are also presented to help us correctly complete our homework assignments while in classroom Earth.

I am spending a little extra time on this subject because this can be controversial with Course students. Some parts of the Course imply that it doesn't matter what seemed to happen, it didn't really happen, what matters is getting back Home. I agree with the idea, but I don't completely agree with the method. I prefer the approach noted here from the Text, Chapter 22:

> "Let us look straight at how this error came about,
> for here lies buried the heavy anchor that seems to
> keep the fear of God in place, immovable and solid

as a rock. While this remains, so will it seem to be."
(ACIM: T-22.VI.10:7-8)

This brings me to my reasoning for exploring the step-by-step sequence of the Old Original Perceived Separation, the OOPS.

1. Understanding that I made an error helps me wrap my mind around why I believe I am in a body on Earth, as well as how I seemed to manifest here.

2. Understanding the step-by-step progression of what seemed to happen helps me comprehend what the Course is talking about. Once I have the basic outline, when I read ACIM, I can put what I'm reading into this framework of understanding, and it makes so much more sense! If I don't have the bigger picture, it can be terribly confusing.

3. Understanding the OOPS helps me look at any occurrences that come up in my current sphere of awareness, acknowledging the ego-based pattern as a symbolic replay of the OOPS.

4. Understanding the progression of wrong decisions that I made, helps me choose again, making better choices moving forward.

All the scenarios of separation represent the first mistake. When I understand the symbolism of the first mistake reflected in what I experience now, it reminds me, "Oh, yeah, this is a rerun of the OOPS." Then I apply True Forgiveness to those current situations. Therefore, I feel it is reasonable to learn about the original error.

Repetition in ACIM and Course-related materials — Repetition is a common theme in the Course. We've been so misled about separating ourselves from God, it takes repetition in slightly different forms to get through to our seemingly separated mind. One way of explaining it will make sense to one person, another way reaches the next person. Sometimes the same person understands it differently on different days. This is part of the Course's holographic nature. It is cohesive and repetitive in its emphatic message that we are not separate, and we never were separate, from God's all-encompassing Love.

Along those same lines, there will be some repetition in the following chapters, but that can be helpful when trying to wrap our minds around the Old Original Perceived Separation. These concepts will be quite new to many readers and it takes repetition to comprehend each step that seemed to land us on Earth, inhabiting bodies. Because a part of our mind ended up backwards and upside-down in the space-time bubble, righting ourselves can be tricky.

Perhaps you have a childhood memory of hanging upside down on monkey bars? Do you remember getting used to the view from that perspective? Then when you jumped down and stood upright, you were dizzy and disoriented. Because we've been stuck upside-down for so long, we believe our inverted viewpoint must be correct.

> "Do you really think it strange that a world in which everything is backwards and upside down arose from this projection of error? It was inevitable."
> (ACIM: T-18.I.6:4-5)

Once we start reorienting ourselves, it still takes time to reverse our upside down viewpoint—and while correcting this, we may experience some disorientation. Repetition helps us understand that we are on the right track.

Changing Fixed Viewpoints — In another illustration of changing viewpoints, the Course alludes to Plato's Allegory of the Cave which describes the resistance that can occur from changing a way of life. In the story, prisoners were in a cave, chained down facing the cave wall in such a way that even their heads could not move. Shadow figures moved along this wall and the prisoners became so accustomed to seeing them, they ardently believed the shadows, and only the shadows, were real.

One of the prisoners was able to free himself. He walked out of the cave and saw a completely expanded, bright and colorful world outside the tight confines that he had been experiencing. He returned to tell the others, "Hey, those shadows are not our reality! What you are seeing is only people walking past a fire which casts shadows on the wall. We've been imprisoned, we could not see the real world outside the cave."

The prisoners did not respond well at all. From their fixed and distorted viewpoint, the shadows were real, and anyone saying otherwise is lying. In fact, the prisoners were so vehemently opposed to the prisoner's expanded viewpoint, they threatened to kill him if he tried to release them from their chains of confinement.

> "Prisoners bound with heavy chains for years, starved and emaciated, weak and exhausted, and with eyes so long cast down in darkness they remember not the light, do not leap up in joy the instant they are

made free. It takes a while for them to understand
what freedom is." (ACIM: T-20.III.9:1-2)

When we dreamed that we separated from God, we imprisoned ourselves with our fixed belief in the separation. Our misperceptions of guilt and fear manifested as chains that we held around ourselves. Some have allowed Spirit to release them and, going ahead of us, they have found the Light. They have come back to tell us that we are grasping onto the chains of fixed beliefs, causing our own confinement. They tell us this need not be. But most of us are afraid to release our chains because we fear change and, in an attempt to feel more secure, we tightly grip our fixed beliefs even more so. We tend to be very 'change averse,' and this passage explains why.

"Many stand guard over their ideas because they want
to protect their thought systems as they are, and
learning means change. Change is always fearful to
the separated, because they cannot conceive of it as
a move towards healing the separation. They always
perceive it as a move toward further separation, because the separation was their first experience of
change. You believe that if you allow no change to
enter into your ego you will find peace." (ACIM: T-
4.I.2:1-4)

The OOPS was the first change that we ever seemed to experience. It did not go well at all, so we believe that any further change will trigger more bad outcomes. We don't remember what living in the endless ecstasy of Heaven's Light feels like, so release can feel threatening because we feel exposed and vulnerable to the unknown.

Many choose to remain in misery, frozen with fear—but

some of us are ready to find a better way. Our will to find a better way is the declaration needed to gently release our chains with help from Spirit. It is done one chain at a time so as not to induce insecurity and the compulsion to grasp at the chain as it is released. This is also why we must be *ready* to release each chain before it is removed. We gently release our false beliefs one at a time with the help of our Teacher, who knows the exact sequence of releases that will best serve us. Learning to trust our Teacher is key. Eventually, we will be free from the self-confinement of our fixed beliefs, all of which arose out of the first error.

The next chapter provides a streamlined overview of the basic steps that seemed to occur during the OOPS. In chapters 8 through 13, we'll explore each step more in-depth. Once the ego dynamics within each step is covered, we'll go over the Holy Spirit's plan to undo the cause of our perceptual problem through True Forgiveness. And that, my friends, is a beautiful thing, indeed! What an inspiring revelation, to learn of our true purpose and function in this world.

CHAPTER 7

The Streamlined Steps of the OOPS

Overview of the Old Original Perceived Separation

The Four Splits of the Mind

THE Old Original Perceived Separation seemed to occur a very long time ago. Before the perceived separation, our awareness was joined in Perfect Oneness with God. Then we began innocently daydreaming and as our mind wandered, we had a thought that was not shared by God. We thought maybe we'd like to be where God is not for just a while. This is impossible in the ultimate reality, but our mind went blank, into a dream-like state. Then a part of the mind began to generate false perceptions of separation.

The original tiny, mad idea did not start out as an intention to separate from God. *The Disappearance of the Universe* explains that it was like a child playing with matches. The child didn't intend to burn the house down, he just wanted to see what happened if he made a little spark with the match. Then, things went downhill from that tiny little spark of an idea.

The cascading reactions that emerged from the tiny, mad idea of separation seemed to cause a series of splits in a part of our mind. With each split, we forgot the previous circumstances, as explained by Arten in DU: "Whenever the mind divides, its new condition is reality to it—its former condition is denied and forgotten." In the dream of separation, this forgetting-what-came-before at each decision-point caused us great confusion.

1st Split = Conscious Perceiver — From Oneness Into twoness

From Perfect Oneness we had a passing idea that we wanted to try something different on our own. Our creative powers unintentionally obliged, and a part of the mind seemed to split, seeming to become separate from Oneness. In this new situation, perception emerged, and we dreamed that we were experiencing twoness: Heaven and us.

2nd Split = Split Consciousness — the ego and the Holy Spirit

It is important to note that God did not join us in our deluded dream of separation, but God's Voice, the Holy Spirit, Called to us to return to Oneness. We forgot our One Mind, then our consciousness split into two ways of perceiving: the ego—our wrong-mind's belief in separation, and the Holy Spirit—the Voice for God Calling us back.

3rd Split = Our decision to identify with the ego

We then had a choice to: Identify with the ego — or — Identify with the Holy Spirit. We could listen to the ego's enticements that fed our desire to be different, a separate individual, even more special than Oneness — or — We could have listened to the Holy Spirit's Call to return to our Home in Perfect Oneness. Not knowing the serious ramifications, we chose the ego but we instantly regretted it, feeling an impending sense of isolation.

4th Split = The making of the world

The ego would have disappeared if we woke up and went back to God, so to keep us from going back to our Source right then and there, the ego made us believe that we had defiantly usurped God's Authority, which made us feel guilty. Then it threatened us with God's impending punishment for tearing a part of Heaven away, which made us extremely fearful. Then the ego offered us a place to hide from our overwhelming guilt and our intense fear of God. Through projection, the multiverse—and our world within it—was manufactured by the ego, providing a space-time bubble in which to 'hide' from God.

The Separation Never Happened—Though it can be difficult for us to understand, there is an important point about this split-mind event: It never actually happened. There is not, and never was, any separation whatsoever. Every perception of separation is a false illusion and impossible in the ultimate reality of Heaven. In the part of the mind that fell asleep, we have amnesia, and we've blocked the memory of our True Self which is safe at Home in God—now, forever, and for always. This is why the Introduction to the Course states: "Nothing real can be threatened. Nothing unreal exists. Herein lies the Peace of God."

THE STREAMLINED STEP-BY-STEP CONSEQUENCES OF CHOOSING THE EGO

The ego's accusations of guilt, which induced the fear of God

1. *The ego's Guilt Accusation* — After identifying with the ego, we became lost in the dream of separation from God. We felt completely alone and vulnerable. The ego knew if we changed our mind, woke up and went back to God, it would disappear. This is because the ego is simply our own thought of separation run amok in our mind. For its very survival, the ego wanted to keep us separate from God. It convinced us that we attacked our Creator, usurping God's Authority by tearing a part of Heaven away.

2. *Our Guilt Reaction* — We believed the ego's accusations that we had sinned against God. Horrible feelings of guilt and regret loomed over us.

3. *The ego Threatened God's Wrathful Punishment*—Because we believed we separated from God, the ego tormented us with threats of "Almighty God's merciless punishment for our 'unforgivable sin' of separation."

4. *Our Inescapable Fear of God* — We believed the ego's threats of punishment for attacking God's authority. Due to our intense guilt about the separation, and our terrifying fear of God's wrath, we felt inescapably vulnerable because God is All-Powerful.

The ego convinced us to hide from God and project our guilt outward

5. *The ego's Plan to Hide from God* — The ego dreamed up

a solution: Escape punishment by hiding from God in a completely separate realm that God supposedly cannot enter.

6. *Our Decision to Hide from God* — Our guilt and fear made us feel vulnerable. We were desperate, willing to do anything or go anywhere to escape our intolerable guilt and fear of God's wrath. This compelled us to agree with the ego to hide from God.

7. *The ego's 'Solution' of Projection* — The ego's solution to 'help' us escape our intense guilt and fear was to use the incredible creative force of our mind to miscreate our multiverse in an explosive outward projection. Our sleeping mind was projected into the space-time bubble where we could believe we were separate from God's terrifying wrath.

8. *Bodies Were Invented* — In dreams of the OOPS, our split mind believed Oneness had been shattered into trillions of fragments. Then the ego devised an even more isolating construct for us to hide in: Bodies. We seem to inhabit our bodies as a solid wall of defense against God. In the body, we experience a sphere of consciousness where we believe we have escaped God's wrath.

The ego's scheme to keep our guilt and fear unconscious

9. *Repression of Unconscious Guilt and Fear* — This is a critical aspect of the ego's plan for escape. It arranged for the giant ball of guilt, fear and regret to be stored in our unconscious so we are not usually aware of it. Like an iceberg, the tip above water can be understood as our consciousness; the submerged portion is our unconscious guilt complex, which is a massive accumulation of our agonizing shame. However, we are not aware of this underlying guilt complex, because it is being held at bay, below our conscious awareness. This is very important to understand: We do not notice this guilt in our awareness, so we do not realize the magnitude of the guilt and fear that lies hidden in our unconscious mind.

10. *Repressed Guilt and Fear arises into Our Awareness*— Sometimes chunks of the submerged unconscious guilt float to the surface into our consciousness. The sickening feeling of our hidden guilt and fear finding us is intolerable. Sometimes people are so overwhelmed with the pain of guilt, they try to escape their misery through suicide. To keep us stuck in the body, the ego invented another device to avoid those surfacing guilt feelings.

11. *Projection Casts Guilt and Fear Onto 'Others'*—There is only One Child of God who is eternally One with God, but the wrong-minded split consciousness seemed to divide and subdivide trillions of times over. In the dream-turned-nightmare, we are convinced by the ego that there are countless 'others' from whom we are separate and apart. Since we feel compelled to escape the misery of our guilt and fear, the ego enables us to unconsciously project our guilt and fear onto those 'others.' The ego convinces us we can escape our self-inflicted guilt by casting it away from ourselves. But there is no 'other' to cast anything upon. What we see as 'other' in the world is only a distorted reflection of our own fractured self. Again, this is absolutely key to understanding the dynamic of our lives here on Earth.

12. *Blame 'Others' Who Behave Badly, Not Us* — Whenever we see something happen in the world that we label as 'bad,' that is actually our own guilt and fear we wanted to get rid of, which we denied and projected outward onto others. We are

not consciously aware that the 'bad' behavior or event is our own guilt and fear we unconsciously projected onto someone else. We firmly believe 'they' did it, they are to blame, and we are justified in our accusations and judgment against them.

13. *Punish 'Them' Because 'They' Were Bad* — We are convinced by the ego that 'they' did something awful, we are their victim, and thus 'they' should be punished. Then we feel vicariously relieved of our guilt, as 'their' punishment seems to alleviate the need for God to punish us for attacking our Source and irrevocably tearing away a piece of Heaven.

The ego's tactics that keep us enmeshed in the script

14. *Threats of Disaster* — In our dream of separation, sometimes there is no 'other' to blame, but we experience looming fear from circumstances 'beyond our control,' such as: cancer, diabetes and viruses; or war and nuclear attacks; or earthquakes, hurricanes, and rogue asteroids. These are all artificial ego constructs projected outward to keep us in the victim role, at the mercy of a merciless, unstable world.

Those diseases and man-made or 'natural disasters' are 'evidence' to prove that we are weak and vulnerable victims of uncertainty. These dangers symbolize our intense guilt and fear of God's retribution, lurking deep within our unconscious mind, which constantly threatens to attack us. As long as the unconscious mind wallows in self-conflict, this accumulated guilt and fear will be denied and projected outward into the world.

15. *Distractions Keep Us Distracted* — In our dream of separation, we seem to subsist in our bodies on this planet, struggling and striving, trying to survive until our bodies die.

In the meantime, the ego plays out its scripts with a seemingly endless parade of threats, traumas and dramas. When one seems to be resolved, another comes up. These preoccupations serve to distract us from asking WHY we are here, preventing us from discovering the truth about God's all-encompassing Love for us. The last thing the ego wants is for us to find out that we are the innocent, beloved and PERFECT Child of God. So the ego continues to invent distractions—myriad scenarios of separation, all symbolizing the Old Original Perceived Separation.

16. *We Continually Seek Substitutions for God's Love* — Even though we never lost God's Love, we put up barriers in our separated mind, blocking God's all-encompassing Love from our awareness. Hiding inside the walls of our wrong-mind, our isolated-inner-self is so small and lonely, it seems that finding Love within our little self is an impossibility. Consequently, the ego directs us to seek outside ourselves in the external world. The ego entices us to seek for Love of some kind to try to fill the void; surely some thing, some body, or some place can provide the lasting Love and happiness we seek. The ego's 'seek but do not find' strategy is designed to fail every time because everything in the externally manifested world is impermanent, so any substitutions for God's Love will not last. There is no substitute for God's Love, and there is no need to seek outside ourselves to find it.

The Atonement — The Holy Spirit's Plan of Salvation

17. *The Holy Spirit is the Still, Small Voice that Calls to Us from our Innermost Self* — In our dream of separation, in order to hear the Call of the Holy Spirit in our right-mind, we Ask

Spirit for help, then Pause, becoming still, being receptive and Listening. In this way, we allow messages to gently speak to our heart. They may emerge in the form of words, feelings, memories, physical sensations, etc. It takes practice to Pause and Listen to the still, small Voice, yet when we do become attuned to it, the Voice becomes stronger, providing even more clarity.

18. *Practicing True Forgiveness is our Function and Purpose* — As we hear and follow Spirit's messages, we are guided through events that bring our unconscious guilt and fear into our conscious mind. Through this communication link, we become more aware of the repeating symbolic patterns of our upsets, grievances, and fears. When we look at them with Spirit and ask to see them differently, the false aspects are dispelled and the Truth shines through into our mind a bit more each time. Practicing True Forgiveness of our false perceptions is our true function and purpose in this world.

19. *Allowing the nightmare of separation to be replaced with a gentle dream of peace* — Once we understand what our perceived upsets, grievances and fears are for—which is to use True Forgiveness to remove layers of guilt and fear from the unconscious mind—our peace of mind becomes more consistent. The Holy Spirit knows the best sequence for removing all of the unconscious guilt and fear from all the separated minds. We trust Spirit to transform our nightmare of separation into a gentle dream of Perfect peace.

20. *Once the fragments of the Christ Mind join as One, God takes the final step of salvation* — Through performing our function of True Forgiveness in this world, we learn that anyone and anything we regard as separate cannot possibly be

separate. We transfer our learning and carry it over to any encounter or thought, using the Golden Rule as a constant gauge for our thoughts and practices.

Knowing there is no 'other,' we are joyous in our reconciliation with every being, reuniting as the innocent and perfect Child of God. In this joined and peaceful state of mind, our whole mind is ready to join with God's Love. We have no fear of God and know no guilt or fear of any kind. Finally, there is nothing to block the purest experience of God's all-encompassing Love. At that point God is able to take the final step, warmly embracing all of us into the Oneness that is eternal Essence.

CHAPTER 8

Detailed Explanation of Each Stage
of the Imagined Separation

THE NEXT several chapters cover the steps of the Old Original Perceived Separation again, but more in-depth. For each of the steps, three features have been added:
- ACIM quotes describing what seemed to happen.
- Commentary on the concept and a simple metaphor to make each step more relatable in everyday terms.
- An ACIM quote conveying a healing message, reminding us that no matter how dire the situation seems to be, we always have the choice of reversal at each step along the way.

It is usually best to read ACIM quotes within the context of the section and chapter, but the intention here is to keep these descriptions as basic as they can be. Many other quotes within the Course echo those that are included here, and the key words can be researched through the FIP or COA's digital search engines.

On a conceptual note, keep in mind that the OOPS cannot be fully understood because the Oneness of God is ineffable and the whole 'separation' never actually happened. A part of the Christ mind is only dreaming that it has happened. [See

The Little Hindrance, (ACIM: T-26.V), to learn more about this concept.] This ties our hands a bit when trying to describe 'what didn't happen' in the dream, so we cannot get too literal. The Course explains in so many ways, that this is all a dream-turned-nightmare, but in the upcoming descriptions, it gets cumbersome to repeat this too frequently. So, if I talk about something in the following chapters as if it has actually happened, please bear in mind, the whole kit-and-kaboodle has been generated by the mind that thought it separated and is dreaming up scenarios of separation.

In addition, the metaphors are meant to put each step into relatable terms, but none of the metaphors will fully represent each concept. It is best not to analyze every single word and detail here, or in the Course, because it is not meant to be learned in that way. Understanding emerges with time and experience, rather than by intellectualizing the content. Let's begin with this simple, yet powerful passage from *A Course in Miracles*:

> "Your mind is one with God's. Denying this and thinking otherwise has held your ego together, but has literally split your mind." (ACIM: T-4.IV.2:7-8)

The Four Splits of the Mind

To review, the Old Original Perceived Separation (The OOPs), seemed to occur a long time ago. Before the perceived separation, our mind was joined in Perfect Oneness with God, then we began innocently daydreaming. Then we had a thought that was not shared by God—the tiny, mad idea of separation. This seemed to cause a series of splits to occur in a part of our mind. And with each split, we forgot the previous circumstances. This forgetting-what-came-before at each decision point caused us great confusion. The thought of separation from God seemed to cause this series of splits in a part of our mind.

1ˢᵗ Split = Conscious Perceiver — We forgot we are an integral part of Perfect Oneness

> "Consciousness, the level of perception, was the first split introduced into the mind after the separation, making the mind a perceiver rather than a creator. Consciousness is correctly identified as the domain of the ego. The ego is a wrong-minded attempt to perceive yourself as you wish to be, rather than as you are." (ACIM: T-3.IV.2:1-3)

When we knew we were connected to everything as One, there were no contrasts, comparisons, degrees or levels. Inventing twoness introduced inevitable points of contention. In Oneness, everything is always equal and interconnected. As a perceiver, we looked askance from the twoness, and something seemed to be 'here' and something seemed to be 'there.' From that vantage point, comparing 'here' and 'there' was unavoidable. Within this dream of dualistic perception, we then developed the compulsion to identify and enhance contrasts: 'I' am here and the 'other' is over there. Even if the two were identical, the vantage point would cause the belief in differences.

Comparing differences between 'I' and the 'other' started devolving into competition between the two, dividing them further. God could not join in this desire for opposing existences, because God's all-encompassing Love is the equal eternal Essence of everything, everywhere.

"Love is one. It has no separate parts and no degrees; no kinds nor levels, no divergencies and no distinctions. It is like itself, unchanged throughout. It never alters with a person or a circumstance. It is the Heart of God, and also of His Son." (ACIM: W-127.1:3-7)

2ND SPLIT = Split Consciousness — The wrong-mind = ego or the right-mind = Holy Spirit

"The separation is merely another term for a split mind. The ego is the symbol of separation, just as the Holy Spirit is the symbol of peace." (ACIM: T-5.III.9:3-4)

In the second split, two choices became available to us. We were being Called Home by the Holy Spirit, but in the split-part of that perceived separation, there was already a desire and a goal to become more special and better than the 'other.' Our reaction in the second split was a desire to be seen and recognized as more important than the Oneness that is God. This seemed to be the only way to maintain the split. Then all the cascading effects unfolded from this desire for specialness.

"The Holy Spirit links the other part—the tiny, mad desire to be separate, different and special — to the Christ, to make the oneness clear to what is really one." (ACIM: T-25.I.5:5)

Regarding the connotation of 'right-mind' and 'wrong-mind," these terms may sound a bit self-righteous, implying something like, "I am so important because I'm using my right-mind." Or, trying to make someone wrong by saying "He is doing a bad thing because he is using his wrong-mind."

There may be a tendency to label 'right' and 'wrong' from a judgmental standpoint. This is not the intention when these terms are used in the Course.

> "The term 'right-mindedness' is properly used as the correction for 'wrong-mindedness,' and applies to the state of mind that induces accurate perception." (ACIM: T-3.IV.4:3)

The wrong-mind is the part of the mind that was simply mistaken about being separate from God. The wrong-mind has made an error that can be corrected. The right-mind is the peaceful part of the mind that perceives accurately because it listens to the Holy Spirit's healing message of Oneness.

A metaphor that I have found helpful for my understanding of the two choices available to us during the OOPS, is that we cannot ride two horses at the same time. The imagery for this metaphor helps the contrasting concepts make sense. Imagine what it would be like trying to ride two horses at the same time—it isn't possible to sit in both saddles. It's also pretty evident which horse I would prefer to ride. The ego's horse is tightly wound, it's unpredictable and tends to bolt when least expected—then I'm getting carried away along with it. Best to dismount as soon as possible!

Now imagine what it's like riding the Holy Spirit's horse. Gentle, peaceful, even-tempered, completely trustworthy at all times—and this horse knows the way Home! Yes please, I would like to ride this horse.

In the second split of the mind, two mutually exclusive thought systems became available to us, one completely false and the other completely True. We could not ride both of those horses at the same time.

"The mind can be right or wrong, depending on the voice to which it listens. Right-mindedness listens to the Holy Spirit, forgives the world, and through Christ's vision sees the real world in its place." (ACIM: C-1.5:1-2)

3ᴿᴰ Sᴘʟɪᴛ = **We decided to identify with the ego**

"We have seen that there are only two parts of your mind. One is ruled by the ego, and is made up of illusions. The other is the home of the Holy Spirit, where truth abides. There are no other guides but these to choose between, and no other outcomes possible as a result of your choice but the fear that the ego always engenders, and the love that the Holy Spirit always offers to replace it." (ACIM: W-66.7:2-5)

In the OOPS, we thought we might like to try something apart from God. We had no idea what that meant. And we did not read the fine print of the ego's 'binding contract.' Once we made the choice, we believed there was no going back. Chapter 8 of the Text refers to the Parable of the Prodigal Son to describe the third split.

"Listen to the story of the prodigal son, and learn what God's treasure is and yours: This son of a loving father left his home and thought he had squandered everything for nothing of any value, although he had not understood its worthlessness at the time. He was ashamed to return to his father, because he thought he had hurt him. Yet when he came home the father welcomed him with joy, because the son himself was his father's treasure. He wanted nothing else." (ACIM: T-8.VI.4:1-4)

We are God's Prodigal Child. In the OOPS, we chose the ego and we decided to strike out on our own, believing we could do better than Perfect Oneness. It did not go well. We made an error, but that's all it was. In every moment of our dream of self-exile, we can reverse the effects, by choosing the Holy Spirit instead.

> "In every difficulty, all distress, and each perplexity, Christ calls to you and gently says, 'My brother, choose again.'" (ACIM: T-31.VIII.3:2)

4ᵗʰ Sᴘʟɪᴛ = **The making of the World**

> "You may be surprised to hear how very different is reality from what you see. You do not realize the magnitude of that one error. It was so vast and so completely incredible that from it a world of total unreality had to emerge. What else could come of it? Its fragmented aspects are fearful enough, as you begin to look at them. But nothing you have seen begins to show you the enormity of the original error, which seemed to cast you out of Heaven, to shatter knowledge into meaningless bits of disunited perceptions, and to force you to make further substitutions. That was the first projection of error outward. The world arose to hide it, and became the screen on which it was projected and drawn between you and the truth." (ACIM: T-18.I.5:1—6:2)

In the fourth split of the mind, the ego projected the sleeping part of our mind that believed it separated into a place that we believed would shield us from God. This brings us to a key concept that is delivered quite early in the Workbook as Lesson 14 and its meaning is profound.

"God did not create a meaningless world." (ACIM:
W-14.6:8)

Our world is Earth, but it is also the multiverse. What we would call 'all of creation.' However, this space-time bubble is actually a miscreation which occurred with the fourth split of the mind.

Now for a big insight that made me very happy, but might make people with a strong biblical connection not very happy. Contrary to all the stories we have heard all our lives, this imperfect world, Earth and the multiverse, was not created by God. As the Course explains, God, Who is Perfect, cannot and would not create the imperfect. This world is undeniably imperfect. When learning this critical concept, these insights deeply resonated with me, and I knew this was a total game-changer for me. Finally, the WHY was beginning to come into focus as these pivotal puzzle pieces fell into place!

"Reality is ultimately known without a form, unpictured and unseen." (ACIM: T-27.III.5:2)

Like the Holodeck on *Star Trek Next Generation*, the ego programmed a world that plays out endless scenarios of separation from God. All of the scenarios symbolically represent the playing out of the OOPS. We stepped into the holodeck and as the door closed, the exit disappeared behind us, then we became lost in the programming. We got carried away in the ego's script. Because the experiences felt so realistic, we forgot they weren't real. For eons, we've believed that we have been living actual lives within the realistic yet artificial simulation that the ego programmed for us.

"Perception selects, and makes the world you see.
It literally picks it out as the mind directs." (ACIM:
T-21.V.1:1-2)

If this seems far-fetched, just think back to the last movie or TV series you watched where you physically tensed up when there was a fight scene, or you cried during a sad part, or you laughed at something quirky in the show. That show we get so caught-up in is nothing but a hoax. Those are actors on a set, reading a script. To get perspective on this, try searching YouTube for production bloopers of your favorite show. There are dozens of crewmembers standing just out of camera-view to ensure the illusion of a storyline is produced. The movie or TV series is fake, but we easily get carried away in it as if it were real.

If it seems preposterous to think that our world is a simulation, consider what scientists have discovered about the most fundamental building blocks of the multiverse—they aren't there. No material substance can be found within the tiniest particles of 'matter.' There is mostly empty space between electrons and the nuclei of atoms. Nuclei contain protons and neutrons, and all the atomic components are made of energetic fields; nothing in material form can be isolated. Matter isn't matter! Our experience in form is not really form.

Inside the space-time bubble, energy temporarily appears in the form of matter. $E = mc^2$ is Energy = mass times the speed of light squared. In an equation, the equality must be reversible, therefore, *mass* times the speed of light squared = Energy! Seemingly tangible objects in this world have been proven to be made up of energy. However, as explained in Gary Renard's books, even energy is false. In the space-time bubble, the ego manipulates energy to manifest our thoughts into tangible objects that we believe are real. In ACIM, whenever the word 'made' or 'make' is used, it nearly always refers to the ego's false illusions—all of which are temporary. When 'create' or 'extend' is used, it refers only to God's creative powers—anything that is created is eternal and changeless. One of the keys to understanding this whole hoax called 'the world' is that the ego 'made' this temporary illusion that is blocking our awareness of God's eternal, all-encompassing Love.

"Beyond the body, beyond the sun and stars, past everything you see and yet somehow familiar, is an arc of golden light that stretches as you look into a great and shining circle. And all the circle fills with light before your eyes. The edges of the circle disappear, and what is in it is no longer contained at all. The light expands and covers everything, extending to infinity forever shining and with no break or limit anywhere. Within it everything is joined in perfect continuity. Nor is it possible to imagine that anything could be outside, for there is nowhere that this light is not…Here is the memory of what you are; a part of this, with all of it within, and joined to all as surely as all is joined in you." (ACIM: T-21.I.8:1—9:3)

The Separation Never Happened

"Your starting point is truth, and you must return to your Beginning. Much has been 'seen' since then, but nothing has really happened. Your Self is still in peace, even though your mind is in conflict." (ACIM: T-3.VII.5:6-8)

The following story symbolically re-enacts what we thought happened, but did not actually happen.

One day, when my daughter was about four, we were shopping at our local grocery store. While Miranda was strolling along by my side, she was daydreaming, not thinking anything in particular. Suddenly, she looked up from her daydream and she couldn't see me. I was right behind her, but she didn't look there. She looked straight ahead, to the left and right, but she could not find me. She panicked, then she yelled for me and started running. I called her and tried to catch up, but she was running out of sheer fear and I couldn't reach her. Because she was yelling for me, she couldn't hear me calling her. Finally, she paused, not knowing which way to run. It was just long enough for me to catch up to her. And let me tell you, I wrapped her up in my arms, and hugged her so tight. I assured her, "I'm here, Miranda. I didn't leave you, I was right behind you the whole time. I love you and I will never leave you."

When I was reading *The Disappearance of the Universe*, this memory came to mind many times. I knew Miranda's belief that she was lost and alone symbolized our erroneous belief that we were separated from God. When we imagined the separation, we thought we did something wrong, and that we were abandoned by God, but it never happened. We were the ones who made up the idea, and feeling intolerably vulnerable, we panicked and put up the false barriers in our mind. In the imagined space-time bubble, we left God, God never left us! And because of free will, we must be the ones to choose to let go of our false beliefs in separation. If God removed our false barriers before we were ready to let them go, we would believe our 'protective' barriers were being taken away from us and we would freak-out in mortal terror.

"You are the dreamer of the world of dreams. No other cause it has, nor ever will. Nothing more fearful than an idle dream has terrified God's Son, and made him think that he has lost his innocence, denied his Father, and made war upon himself. So fearful is the dream, so seeming real, he could not waken to reality without the sweat of terror and a scream of mortal fear, unless a gentler dream preceded his awaking, and allowed his calmer mind to welcome, not to fear, the Voice that calls with love to waken him; a gentler dream, in which his suffering was healed and where his brother was his friend. God willed he waken gently and with joy, and gave him means to waken without fear." (ACIM: T-27.VII.13:1-5)

CHAPTER 9

The Step-by-Step Consequences of Choosing the Ego

"Every (illusion) the ego makes involves a contradiction in terms, because the mind is split between the ego and the Holy Spirit, so that whatever the ego makes is incomplete and contradictory." (ACIM: T-3.VI.7:4)

Even though "Nothing real can be threatened, nothing unreal exists, herein lies the peace of God," the split-mind believed that we separated. The ego misused the creative power of our mind, to 'make' shifting images that depict all kinds of scenarios of separation from our Source. To be clear, the ego devised experiences of separation, but they are not real.

"Do not be afraid of the ego. It depends on your mind, and as you made it by believing in it, so you can dispel it by withdrawing belief from it." (ACIM: T-7.VIII.5:1-2)

The ego is simply our own belief in separation, not an entity itself. When we withdraw our belief in separation, the ego is simply dispelled.

"As darkness disappears in light, so ignorance fades away when knowledge dawns." (ACIM: T-14.VII.1:6)

There is no need to attack the ego to subdue it. In fact, attacking it would only perpetuate our belief in it. The Course teaches us that as we withdraw our belief in the illusions that the ego made, it simply disappears. That is what the miracle is for, to shine the Light of Truth into the dark and scary world we made, causing the false to disappear and the Truth to shine forth in the world.

"Children perceive frightening ghosts and monsters and dragons, and they are terrified. Yet if they ask someone they trust for the meaning of what they perceive, and are willing to let their own interpretations go in favor of reality, their fear goes with them. When a child is helped to translate his 'ghost' into a curtain, his 'monster' into a shadow, and his 'dragon' into a dream, he is no longer afraid, and laughs happily at his own fear. You, my child, are afraid of your brothers and of your Father and of yourself. But you are merely deceived in them." (ACIM: T-11. VIII.14:1-2)

The ego's accusations of guilt, which induced the fear of God

Going over the Steps of The OOPS in more detail sheds light on the dynamics of our false perceptions so we know how to avoid repeating the pattern moving forward.

Once we chose the ego, our True Home was forgotten. The new circumstances wiped-out our knowledge that we are an integral part of God's all-encompassing Love. The Holy Spirit's Voice of guidance was always with us, but we could not hear it over the ego's loud accusations.

The ego's Guilt Accusation

The ego had a strong instinct to survive by any means necessary and it feared it would disappear if we returned to Oneness. Consequently, the ego's means of survival was to keep us separate from God. In order to ensure that we would not go Home with the Holy Spirit, the ego suddenly accused us of attacking God and usurping God's Authority. The ego convinced us that by separating from God, we tore a part of Heaven away, irrevocably offending God.

> "The ego is quite literally a fearful thought. However ridiculous the idea of attacking God may be to the sane mind, never forget that the ego is not sane. It represents a delusional system, and speaks for it. Listening to the ego's voice means that you believe it is possible to attack God, and that a part of Him has been torn away by you." (ACIM: T-5.V.3:7-10)

I have distinct childhood memories of the awful sensation of feeling guilty. Do you, too? Think back to how it felt. I remember when I got caught doing something I wasn't supposed to, I was practically paralyzed with shame. In my mind I felt an ever-widening chasm of guilt opening up inside me. The echoing accusations of guilt made me feel intolerably vulnerable. I felt like the whole world knew I had done this 'bad' thing and I believed I would feel that humiliating sense of guilt and shame forever.

I gradually learned that the guilt does subside, but it certainly could recur at any moment, should something else equally as shameful be revealed. The subsiding of the guilty feeling does not mean that the shame has gone away, it has just submerged into my unconscious—the shameful memory can return to haunt me at any moment.

These episodes of guilt-mongering are part of the ego's strategy to keep us entangled in illusions. I still get sickening stabs of guilt as my mind replays memories of hurtful things I have done. They are still there, held in suspended animation until the memory is re-activated. The ego periodically brings up random accusations of guilt, just to keep me captivated by the illusion. Before I read the Course, I would cringe at my shameful memories surfacing from the depths. My stomach would involuntarily lock up, and I could only wait for the nauseating feeling to go away. Out of sight, but not out of mind.

Now I recognize the ego's guilt accusation as a True Forgiveness opportunity. Whenever a guilt episode confronts me, I Ask Spirit, Pause & Listen to help me see my guilty memory differently. Then Spirit gives me a healing message and the shift in perception releases my icky-guilt feeling, which gives me a comforting sense of relief.

> "If you will lay aside the ego's voice, however loudly it may seem to call; if you will not accept its petty gifts that give you nothing that you really want; if you will listen with an open mind…then you will hear the mighty Voice of truth, quiet in power, strong in stillness, and completely certain in Its messages." (ACIM: W-106.1:1)

Our Guilt Reaction

In the part of the mind that seemed to split, we believed the ego's accusations. We believed we sinned against God. Feelings of intense unforgivable guilt, regret, and isolation loomed over us.

"…the mind which believes it has a separate will that can oppose the Will of God, also believes it can succeed. That this can hardly be a fact is obvious. Yet, that it can be believed as fact is equally obvious. And herein lies the birthplace of guilt. Who usurps the place of God and takes it for himself now has a deadly 'enemy.' And he (believes he) must stand alone in his protection, and make himself a shield to keep him safe from fury that can never be abated, and vengeance that can never be satisfied." (ACIM: M-17.5:4-9)

Our guilt reaction is like a fish being attracted to bait on a hook. An expert fisherman knows just how to entice the fish to take the bait. He watches from his boat, through the surface of the water, as the fish approaches the bait and nibbles at it. Tipping the fishing pole slightly, the fisherman makes the bait look as if it is alive and about to swim away. "Oh, no," the fish worries, "It's going to get away!" Watching for just the right moment when the fish gulps down the bait, a sudden pull of the line sets the hook deep into the mouth of the fish.

With a similar technique, the ego lures us in, enticing us with its guilt-bait. How often have we taken emotional-bait from the news, social media, our friends or family? And how many times have we gone back for more? I have certainly taken my share of guilt-bait, getting snagged by ego-hooks over the years—oh yes—and I still do. However, I am learning to be more cautious when I feel lured in. I'm sometimes tempted to nibble, but as soon as I sense there's something fishy about this tempting morsel with strings attached, I am learning to pass it by.

In the Old Original Perceived Separation, we took the ego's guilt-bait, hook, line and sinker. We reacted exactly as the ego expected, swimming right into the trap. There we were, on the hook, believing the lies that the ego expertly baited us with. However, as hopeless as our situation seemed to be, the Truth could have set us free; and it still will set us free.

"Without guilt, the ego has no life, and God's Son <u>is</u> without guilt." (ACIM: T-13.I.2:5)

The ego Threatened God's Wrathful Punishment

Once we took the ego's guilt-bait, we were on the hook. We believed the ego's accusations of guilt, then we were tormented with the ego's threats of Almighty God's merciless wrath and impending punishment for our 'unforgivable sins.'

- "What else but sin could be the source of guilt, demanding punishment and suffering?" (ACIM: W-259.1:4)
- "For the ego brings sin to fear, demanding punishment." (ACIM: T-19.III.2:2)
- "Guilt, then, is a way of holding past and future in your mind to ensure the ego's continuity. For if what has been will be punished, the ego's continuity is guaranteed." (ACIM: T-13.I.8:6-7)

Here is another twist in the very sketchy plot of the OOPS. The ego accused us of being guilty of the separation, we bought into the guilt, and then, the ego ramped up the drama with another impossible lie. The ego's 'logic' dictates that we did something very, very wrong, and we are very, very guilty. Consequently, the ego tells us that in performing this grave travesty, we committed a terrible 'sin' against God.

In the ego's threatening accusation, a sin is unforgivable, a giant mark on our permanent record. And for committing this heinous crime, we will be punished by God for eternity—*Bwah-ha-ha!*

The ego bids we look at all the terrifying threats of looming doom and gloom surrounding us—great roiling, boiling vats of noxious toxic waste await us. The ego manufactures threats of torture, torment and gnashing of teeth—yet, have you ever noticed, that there seems to be all of those hellish punishments right here on Earth?

Remember the Jewish proverb referenced earlier, 'Hell is distance from God.' The further we believe we are from God, the more hellish is our experience. In the OOPS, the ego's threats of punishment were calculated and targeted to our most vulnerable fears, as this ACIM quote describes.

> "And so they fear the Holy Spirit, and perceive the 'wrath' of God in Him. Nor can they trust Him not to strike them dead with lightning bolts torn from the 'fires' of Heaven by God's Own angry Hand. They do believe that Heaven is hell, and are afraid of love." (ACIM: T-25.VIII.6:3-5)

The ego's threats were convincing, and being identified with the ego, we believed them. We unconsciously continue to believe that God is out-to-get-us to punish us for our 'sins.' Keep in mind, one of the tricks of the wrong-mind is to conceal this fear of punishment out of our awareness.

- "The Holy Spirit will help you reinterpret everything that you perceive as fearful, and teach you that only what is loving is true." (ACIM: T-5.IV.1:3)
- "God can no longer be feared, for the mind sees no

cause for punishment." (ACIM: M-12.2:4)

Our Reaction of Inescapable Fear of God

Although in Truth there is no cause for guilt or punishment, during the OOPS we felt inescapably vulnerable. We were afraid because God is All-Powerful and the little part that we thought we tore away from Heaven was tiny and helpless. We were paralyzed by our mortal fear of God.

"The unforgiving mind is torn with doubt, confused about itself and all it sees; afraid and angry, weak and blustering, afraid to go ahead, afraid to stay, afraid to waken or to go to sleep, afraid of every sound, yet more afraid of stillness; terrified of darkness, yet more terrified at the approach of light." (ACIM: W-121.3:1)

This fear reaction that we had to the ego's deception was intense, instinctual, and inescapable. We still harbor this insidious fear of God in our wrong-mind. Our fear of God has been depicted in so many ways over the eons. Various institutional religions, in particular, have capitalized on our deep-seated fearful beliefs. For example, certain dualistic aspects of the Bible incur plenty of those fears, as do many religious texts. Here is just a sampling of some of the fearful messages included in both the Old Testament and the New Testament:

- Romans 1:18 - For the wrath of God is revealed from heaven against all ungodliness and unrighteousness of men, who hold the truth in unrighteousness.
- John 3:36 - He that believeth on the Son hath everlasting life: and he that believeth not the Son shall not see life; but the wrath of God abideth on him.

- Isaiah 26:21 - For, behold, the LORD cometh out of his place to punish the inhabitants of the Earth for their iniquity: the Earth also shall disclose her blood, and shall no more cover her slain.
- Ezekiel 25:17 - And I will execute great vengeance upon them with furious rebukes; and they shall know that I am the LORD, when I shall lay my vengeance upon them.
- Nahum 1:2-6 - God is jealous, and the LORD revengeth; the LORD revengeth, and is furious; the LORD will take vengeance on his adversaries, and he reserveth wrath for his enemies.
- Revelation 20:15 - And whosoever was not found written in the book of life was cast into the lake of fire.
- 2 Peter 2:9 - The LORD knoweth how to deliver the godly out of temptations, and to reserve the unjust unto the day of judgment to be punished.
- Matthew 10:28 - And fear not them which kill the body, but are not able to kill the soul: but rather fear him which is able to destroy both soul and body in hell.
- John 15:6 - If a man abide not in me, he is cast forth as a branch, and is withered; and men gather them, and cast them into the fire, and they are burned.
- Hebrews 9:22 - And almost all things are by the law purged with blood; and without shedding of blood is no remission.
- Psalms 7:11 - God judgeth the righteous, and God is angry with the wicked every day.
- Luke 12:5 - But I will forewarn you whom ye shall fear: Fear him, which after he hath killed hath power to cast

into hell; yea, I say unto you, Fear him.

Um, yeah… so there's that…

This simply illustrates the dualistic nature of certain aspects of the Bible. There are also many beautiful and Loving passages in the Bible, such as the following verses, describing the safety and Love of God:

- Psalms 4:28 — I will both lay me down in peace, and sleep: for thou, LORD, only makest me dwell in safety.
- 1 John 4:7 — Beloved, let us love one another: for love is of God; and every one that loveth is born of God, and knoweth God.
- 1 John 4:12 — No man hath seen God at any time. If we love one another, God dwelleth in us, and his love is perfected in us.
- 1 Peter 1:22 — Seeing ye have purified your souls in obeying the truth through the Spirit unto unfeigned love of the brethren, see that ye love one another with a pure heart fervently.
- Colossians 3:14 — And above all these, put on love, which binds everything together in perfect harmony.
- Corinthians 13: 7-8 — Love bears all things, believes all things, hopes all things, endures all things. Love never ends.
- Philippians 4:13 — I can do all things through Christ who strengthens me.
- 1 John 4:16 — We know how much God loves us, and we have put our trust in His love. God is love and all who love live in God and God lives in them.

For every fearful depiction of God, the Bible contains an equally Loving illustration. So which are we supposed to believe? They cannot both be true. These opposing descriptions of God are confusing to say the least. A society that bases its tenets on these highly contradictory thought systems is bound to be dualistic, disparate, and tragically messed-up. Hmm…. And how is that working out for us?

Consequently, while trying to navigate this weirdly incongruent realm, I had to Ask WHY? This is insanity! This world does not make sense! If God is Loving, how can God also be vindictive, jealous, angry, furious, spiteful, and punishing? That does not sound like God to me.

Just like the Bible's contrasting verses, for every 'good' thing in this world, there seems to be an unpleasant 'bad' thing. For all the beauty, equal ugliness seems to lurk around the corner. For all the Love, there seems to be fear. For all the triumphs, there seem to be devastating defeats. On and on the duality rolls along. And we seem to have no choice but to accept it, to tolerate it, and to acquiesce to the way of the world. This is why I have always asked, WHY— Because this 'way of the world' is not Okay.

This is one reason I resonate so deeply with *A Course in Miracles*, because it is certain and completely consistent in its description of God as Pure Love, and nothing else. There is never any question that God is Perfect, that God created us Perfect, and that God Loves us completely and eternally. This is the God of my heart. This feels right to me. It may not seem so from this world's limited perspective, but I know it, I am certain of it from a place in my heart that is not of this world.

"The Son of God is egoless. What can he know of madness and the death of God, when he abides in Him? What can he know of sorrow and of suffering, when he lives in eternal joy? What can he know of fear and punishment, of sin and guilt, of hatred and attack, when all there is surrounding him is everlasting peace, forever conflict-free and undisturbed, in deepest silence and tranquility?" (ACIM: W-pII.12.3:1-4)

CHAPTER 10

The Ego Convinced Us to Hide from God and to Project Our Guilt Outward

The ego's Plan to Hide from God

MEANWHILE, back at the cascading consequences of the OOPS, we were suffering greatly from our decision to listen to the ego. Believing we had torn ourselves away from God, we felt we were all alone and on our own. We were so tiny and helpless under the 'great threat' of God's wrath and impending punishment. Then the ego offered a 'solution' to our paralyzing fear: Hide in a place that God cannot enter; a place separate and away from God, so we can escape punishment.

> "The ego's plan, of course, makes no sense and will not work. By following its plan you will merely place yourself in an impossible situation, to which the ego always leads you." (ACIM: T-9.IV.4:2-3)

Think about what happens when you lift up a rock and look at what's living underneath it. Many varieties of insects might be dwelling there, but once the rock is lifted, they feel vulnerable to attack. Once they are exposed, they don't just sit there, they quickly scurry away with an instinctive need to hide.

Likewise, we felt exposed and intolerably vulnerable when

the ego accused us of offending God and invoking God's wrath and punishment. This fear-inducing tactic ensured we would not listen to or follow the Holy Spirit's Voice calling us Home. Not only would we not run toward God, the ego's lies made us want to run away from God in terror. "Not to worry," claimed the ego, "I have a plan to hide you away from God. Let's scurry away out of sight."

> "There is a kind of experience so different from anything the ego can offer that you will never want to cover or hide it again." (ACIM: T-4.III.5:1)

Our Decision to Hide from God

Our heavy guilt and terrifying fear urged us to hide from God's impending punishment. We were desperate and willing to do anything or go anywhere to escape God's wrath. We decided with the ego to hide from God.

> "It is only in darkness and in ignorance that you perceive the frightening, and shrink away from it to further darkness. And yet it is only the hidden that can terrify, not for what it is, but for its hiddenness."
> (ACIM: T-14.VI.1:3-4)

[Note: I'm going to use a metaphor about ostriches burying their heads in the sand, thinking they are hiding. However, ostriches don't actually do that. They are most likely building a nest, tending to young, keeping cool or gathering food from the ground. My metaphor refers to the stereotypical assumption that they believe they are hiding themselves when they hide their head in the sand. I'll use a little poetic license here, because the imagery of this analogy is helpful!]

When I think of our decision to follow the ego's plan to

hide from God, I picture the image of an ostrich burying its head in the sand. The ostrich looks quite foolish with its head stuck in a hole in the ground and its bum high in the air, believing it has hidden itself.

Now imagine what the bird sees from its perspective from the hole in the ground: Darkness, barriers, nothingness. Nothing from this world can be seen by the ostrich's eyes because its view of the world has been blocked. All it can see is darkness. If it stays there a while, it might fall asleep and start dreaming. Because of its limited viewpoint, it may begin to believe the images that its mind is dreaming up are its 'reality,' but it is only a dream.

Now let's picture ourselves as the ostrich hiding from God. We're upside-down, disoriented, burying our head in a hole. We believe we are hidden from view because our eyes can only see darkness, but it is only our viewpoint that is severely limited. Pretty silly, right? Well, guess what? That's not far off from what we did to ourselves in the OOPS. We wanted to hide, and we believed we went away and hid from God, but we never did. We just convinced ourselves that we did. It's going to take a process to become upright, because when we reverse our inversion, it will seem disorienting.

In addition, when going from a dark and limited viewpoint to an expansive, brightly-lit viewpoint, our eyes will have to adjust to the Light. This is one reason why the Holy Spirit doesn't whisk away our miscreations that are blocking our ability to see the Light of Truth. Imagine sleeping in a dark room, someone walks in, flips on the light-switch and suddenly bright light glares into our eyes. "Gaaa! It's too much, too soon!" we exclaim, as we clamp our eyes shut and rush to cover our eyes to block the light. Turning on the bright light is not helpful, because we become even more focused on resisting and blocking the light.

There must be a better way. Well, I'm glad you asked, because, yes, there is! The Holy Spirit has a plan to help us gradually remove the barriers we have placed to block the Light of Truth. Our barriers are a multi-layered collection of stories symbolizing the desire to be separate from God. These hoarded narratives make up our ego-based identity and include all our goals, beliefs, thoughts, emotions, and false perceptions depicting the separation. This is why it usually takes many True Forgiveness practices to carefully remove those barriers that block the Light of Truth in our mind. This allows the mind to adjust to the Light very gently.

- "A miracle inverts perception, which was upside down before, and thus it ends the strange distortions that were manifest." (ACIM: W-pII.13.2:3)

- "God hides nothing from His Son, even though His Son would hide himself. Yet the Son of God cannot hide his glory, for God wills him to be glorious, and gave him the light that shines in him." (ACIM: T-11. III.5:1-2)

- "In the holy instant, you ask of love only what it offers everyone, neither less nor more. Asking for everything, you will receive it. And your shining Self will lift the tiny aspect that you tried to hide <u>from</u> Heaven straight <u>to</u> Heaven." (ACIM: T-18.VIII.11:4-6)

The ego's 'Solution' of Projection

The ego's solution to escape the self-destructive guilt and fear was to explosively project it outward and away from our-selves. The incredible creative force of our mind was manipu-lated to miscreate a hidey-hole for us—a 'temporal anomaly' known as our multiverse. The sleeping part of our mind was thrown into the bubble, so at the level of consciousness, we believed we were separate from God and had escaped God's terrible wrath.

> "You have made many ideas that you have placed
> between yourself and your Creator, and these beliefs
> are the world as you perceive it. Truth is not absent
> here, but it is obscure." (ACIM: T-11.VII.4:4-5)

So the ego misused the enormously creative powers of our mind to explosively project our fear of God away from us, into a space-time bubble. I think of it like a balloon. When we blow into the balloon, air goes inside, and the edges of the balloon expand. A part of our mind was blown inside the balloon, and from inside this latex balloon, we cannot see beyond that bar-rier. Consequently, from within the balloon, we have a very limited perspective on what is going on outside the balloon. This is why it is not possible to fully explain our ultimate re-ality outside the balloon—we just cannot understand it from our reference points inside the barrier of the balloon.

Let's take a look at everything we believe we know about living within the multiverse. First, we seem to live on the sur-face of a blue planet called Earth. Now pull back a little fur-ther from our perspective on Earth and view the solar system. With the sun in the center, look down from the center to the orbiting planets. How does Earth look now? Yup, it's just a tiny blue dot. Everything that is happening on Earth including traffic jams, headlines in the news, and armed conflicts seem so far away from this vantage point.

Now imagine Earth from the perspective above our Milky Way galaxy. Our solar system is on an arm of the spiral, not too close to the center. From this angle, Earth can't even be seen as a tiny blue dot. Our sun is one among, say, 300 billion stars, so maybe our sun is a teenie-tiny little point of light among billions.

Next, imagine our galaxy among, say, 300 billion galaxies within the cosmos. The Milky Way is just a blurry schmear among billions of nebulae. Now try to view our cosmos as one bubble among, say, 300 billion-ish parallel planes of existence. Imagine a big glob of bubbles forming a network, like a dome of foaming detergent piled-up on a plate.

At this printing, this is the extent of our knowledge of the material world within the multiverse. With our observations, measurements, and mathematical formulae, we believe we have figured out the physical laws of space-time within the balloon, but even those are coming into question as technology advances. And even so, the physical laws of this balloon are not God's Laws of all-encompassing Love.

> "The ego's interpretations of the laws of perception
> are, and would have to be, the exact opposite of the
> Holy Spirit's." (ACIM: T-11.V.14:1)

And where is God within the ego's balloon of space-time? We wanted to hide from God, so we projected ourselves into the balloon. Then because we could not see God within the balloon, we assumed God was not there. Many still believe God is separate from us, which, if you think about it, is a pretty big assumption.

The ego's plan to hide from God, to take all of our guilt and fear and project it away from us, into a multiverse of separation, seems to have worked. The key point is, we believe that it did work, and then we forgot that we were the ones who decided to project ourselves into this escape pod in the first place. We are just so forgetful! But the Holy Spirit has not forgotten us.

> "The ego made the world as it perceives it, but the Holy Spirit, the reinterpreter of what the ego made, sees the world as a teaching device for bringing you home." (ACIM: T-5.III.11:1)

Bodies were invented

Our Oneness seemed to be shattered and scattered into trillions of individual fragments which were projected into the multiverse. Then the ego devised an even more isolating construct for us to hide in: Bodies. We seem to inhabit our bodies as a separated, solid wall of defense against God. In the body, we experience consciousness, and we believe we have escaped both our guilt and our fear of God's wrath.

> "The hope of specialness makes it seem possible God made the body as the prison house that keeps His Son from Him. For it demands a special place God cannot enter, and a hiding place where none is welcome but your tiny self. Nothing is sacred here but unto you, and you alone, apart and separate from all your brothers; safe from all intrusions of sanity upon illusions; safe from God, and safe for conflict everlasting. Here are the gates of hell you closed upon

yourself, to rule in madness and in loneliness your special kingdom, apart from God, away from truth and from salvation." (ACIM: T-24.II.13:1-4)

This quote describing the hope of specialness is an important paragraph from ACIM Chapter 24. Part of the reason the split-mind separated is that once we seemed to split Oneness into twoness, we made comparisons one to the 'other.' We believed the only way to achieve being separate from God was to strive to be more special than God.

Similar to a child acting out to get attention, we started competing with God for hierarchy. We wanted God to pay attention to our specialness. God could not share our idea of separation, however, because there is nowhere that God's all-encompassing Love is not present. In response, the ego insidiously convinced us that, because God did not buy into to the twoness perception, God did not *want* us. In our wounded indignance we rejected God in return.

In our dejected rejection, the ego told us that the body is the 'perfect' place to maintain our specialness and our separation from God. But, in another deceptive distortion, the ego told us that God made the body. The ego convinced us that this is true and insisted that anyone who questions the logic of this lie is guilty of blasphemy. How many have suffered at the level of form for not buying into it? It's ingeniously clever, deviously convoluted, and entirely false.

Here is another thought experiment to help us consider the artificiality of living in a body on the surface of Earth for a few decades. Imagine Earth as a snow-globe floating within the balloon of the multiverse; the parallels are remarkable. With both the Earth and the snow-globe, we find 'snow' and liquid water. The dome of the snow-globe is clear, but it is formed in such a way that it encases the contents, much like our atmosphere. Sometimes Earth's liquid and gases get shaken up with a hurricane or a storm. Then, just like a snow-globe, things tend to settle again.

Imagine the artificial scenes of daily life going on inside the snow-globe. Little plastic houses with tiny lit-up lamp posts and trees lining the street. Little plastic people walking on the sidewalk, and miniature cars parked on either side of the street. Maybe there's a town square with a little courthouse, a library, and a park. We could even imagine moving scenes like the miniature models of towns with country scenery and a train clicking along the tracks, train horn blowing each time it circles 'round the town [Note: As I wrote this, a train horn just echoed in the distance].

What else would be in our snow-globe? We might see a young couple sitting on a swing, holding hands, gazing into each other's eyes. Tiny cars are parked at the drive-in and a movie is playing on the little 'big' screen. On the streets, we see people in their cars with little headlights on, their arms waving back-and-forth to someone walking on the sidewalk. In the distance, we see a field with cattle raising their heads, then lowering them to get a bite of green grass.

Now we notice a circus tent at the edge of town. Can you hear the circus music playing? Families are walking toward the entrance of the tent as light shines from the open tent flap. Next to the tent, a colorful carousel slowly rotates, the horses raise and lower their riders every few seconds.

In our imaginary moving-model-snow-globe, there's a certain set of activities the people do each day. These miniature citizens go through the same motions over and over. Sometimes things get topsy-turvy, the weather gets sloshy, and snow floats down. But it settles soon enough. Just like snow-globe Earth....

While reading the description here, did you find yourself imagining the sights and sounds of the scenes? When you imagined the couple in the swing, did it feel like 'young love' to you? When imagining the people waving and the cattle grazing, did they come to life in your mind? For just a few seconds, did you lose yourself while dreaming-up this imaginary world? Imagination can be powerful, indeed.

Likewise, when we take off in an airplane, we can look down and see all the houses in the neighborhoods. In some of the tiny fenced-off backyards, sunlight glints off blue swimming pools. We see grocery stores with cars pulling in and out of their little parking lots. Then we look toward the downtown area to view the miniature office buildings of varying shapes and sizes. We see the traffic below on little highways and byways. Don't they look like ants following a pheromone trail? When we think of the repeating daily cycles of Earthlings, isn't it a little like the miniature moving model? Do the artificial constructs seem not quite as important when we have elevated our viewpoint high up in the air?

"Sit quietly and look upon the world you see, and tell yourself: 'The real world is not like this. It has no buildings and there are no streets where people walk alone and separate. There are no stores where people buy an endless list of things they do not need. It is not lit with artificial light, and night comes not upon it. There is no day that brightens and grows dim. There is no loss. Nothing is there but shines, and shines forever.'" (ACIM: T-13.VII.1:1-7)

[Note: This whole section, Chapter 13, Section VII The Attainment of the Real World, is relevant to the subject of this world's artificiality.]

The ego's maneuver of projecting the splintered fragments of our consciousness into individual bodies certainly was convincing. It is understandable why most people think life on this Earth, in these bodies, is 'real.' But everything here is temporary, everything tangible decays and dies and will eventually be lost. So for some, the questions keep coming: What am I? What is this for? What is real? How did I get here? Where am I going when my body dies? What's the point? WHY does this world feel so artificial and so wrong? It does not add up.

- "God did not make the body, because it is destructible, and therefore not of the Kingdom. The body is the symbol of what you think you are. It is clearly a separation device, and therefore does not exist." (ACIM: T-6.V-A.2:1-3)

- "Heaven remains your one alternative to this strange world you made and all its ways; its shifting patterns and uncertain goals, its painful pleasures and its tragic joys." (ACIM: W-131.7:1)

CHAPTER 11

The ego's Scheme to Keep our Guilt and Fear Unconscious

BEFORE going over the patterns of repression and projection I want to go over some relevant material that appears in Helen's handwritten notes in the COA version, but is not found in the FIP version. In the first several chapters of the COA, there are mentions of the levels of the split mind: the superconscious, conscious, and subconscious levels.

The superconscious mind retains our awareness of God and it pulls us to come Home to Oneness. The conscious level is what we experience in this world in our everyday lives. The subconscious is divided into two layers. The superficial layer is where our guilt and fear is hidden just out of our conscious awareness, this is often referred to as the 'unconscious.' The deep level of the subconscious houses our powerful miracle impulses which compel us to rejoin with the fragments of the split mind. Sometimes as the miracle impulses of the deep subconscious are rising up into our consciousness, the unconscious guilt layer distorts the message, and we misperceive it as a physical impulse such as a sexual urge to join physically or a compulsive addiction. COA's Chapter 3, Section VI. The Divided Mind, describes some of these concepts. I found this information to be quite helpful in understanding our physical impulses as well as our inborn superconscious pull to return to God. It can also be helpful in understanding the following steps of the OOPS.

Repression of Unconscious Guilt and Fear

In the dream, in a critical aspect of the ego's plan of separation, the ego has arranged for the giant ball of agonizing guilt and fear to be repressed in the unconscious—where it is stored out of our awareness. Like an iceberg, the tip above water can be understood as our consciousness; the unseen submerged portion is our unconscious guilt complex.

> "The circle of fear lies just below the level the body sees, and seems to be the whole foundation on which the world is based. Here are all the illusions, all the twisted thoughts, all the insane attacks, the fury, the vengeance and betrayal that were made to keep the guilt in place, so that the world could rise from it and keep it hidden." (ACIM: T-18.IX.4:2)

Certain aspects of the 1999 movie *The Matrix* illustrate the ego's devious tactics. The plot provides a symbolic depiction of the ego's repression of our guilt and fear. In the movie, people seem to be living in a normal world, going about their lives, repeating the cycles they are supposed to do each day. It all seems so real and so normal. Much like the patterns we repeat each day seem real and normal.

Then Neo, the hero of the movie, is given the option to learn what is really going on behind-the-scenes of the simulated world that people think they are living in. Neo is offered the famous 'red pill' to find out, or the 'blue pill' which would return him to his pre-programmed coma-like existence. After Neo chooses the red pill, the disturbingly dark nature of human existence is revealed to him.

In the dark underworld, Neo discovers that Artificially Intelligent machines have become sentient and have enslaved humans by connecting cables to them and encasing their bodies inside cytoplasmic pods. While their bodies are being drained of energy, a virtual program occupies the minds of the captive humans with a simulated life story. Within their seemingly normal lives, they are completely unaware that they are being parasitized by A.I. machinery.

Likewise, the ego has kept the ugliness of our giant guilt complex at bay by keeping it just out of our awareness. We don't see the horrors of our unconscious with our human eyes, but at the same time, the ego keeps our mind attached to and enslaved by this underlying layer of guilt and fear. One way this is accomplished is by symbolically reminding us of our guilt for the separation in every scenario that plays out within the virtual simulation of life in this world.

> "Each day, and every minute in each day, and every instant that each minute holds, you but relive the single instant when the time of terror took the place of love." (ACIM: T-26.V.13:1)

What we believe we see in this dream world may not seem virtual, but the people of *The Matrix* are convinced their experience is reality, and it definitely is not.

A number of scientists, particularly in the field of quantum physics, are accumulating evidence that the multiverse is a holographic illusion, like pixels in a video game. It is interesting to note that in October 2022, the Nobel Prize for Physics was awarded to three physicists who each contributed to the ability to test and confirm quantum entanglement, which suggests that the universe is non-local and cannot be considered real. Gradually we are learning that this existence is not what we think it is. [See YouTube post titled "How Physicists Proved The Universe Isn't Real — Nobel Prize in Physics 2022 Explained".]

> "This deception makes you fearful because you realize in your heart it is a deception, and you exert enormous efforts to establish its reality. The miracle sets reality where it belongs. Reality belongs only to spirit, and the miracle acknowledges only truth. It thus dispels illusions about yourself, and puts you in communion with yourself and God." (ACIM: T-1.IV.2:2-5)

Repressed Guilt and Fear sometimes rise into our awareness

In the dream state, sometimes chunks of the submerged iceberg of unconscious guilt float to the surface of our consciousness. This causes us great distress, because we think we are successfully hiding from it. The sickening feeling of our guilt and fear surfacing and reflecting back at us is intolerable.

> "(Guilt's) shadow rises to the surface, enough to hold its most external manifestations in darkness, and to bring despair and loneliness to it and keep it joyless. Yet its intensity is veiled by its heavy coverings, and kept apart from what was made to keep it hidden. The body cannot see this, for the body arose from this for its protection, which depends on keeping it not seen. The body's eyes will never look on it. Yet

they <u>will</u> see what it dictates." (ACIM: T-18.IX.4:1-7) Any experience in this world that disturbs our peace of mind, no matter how big or how small, is our unconscious guilt rising into our consciousness. When events or people upset us, we react with any range of emotions, but underneath that reaction, the real reason we are upset is because we're afraid. We believed we were successfully hiding from our guilt and fear —but it found us. The key concept is that we wanted to deny our guilt and fear so it was projected out of our awareness. However, we cannot truly hide from our guilt and fear because at a quantum level, what we believe will be experienced in this world. If we believe we are guilty and we will be punished by God, this will be reflected in our virtual reality.

"Your picture of the world can only mirror what is within." (ACIM: W-73.5:1)

Remember going into a fun-house as a kid? We saw ourselves in the distorted mirrors, but the images did not look like us. The various types of distortions made us look weirdly tall and skinny or absurdly short and wide. As we moved, the image moved, yet our 'self' was nearly unrecognizable to our eyes.

In the OOPS, we followed the ego into a not-so-fun house, completely filled with distorted mirrors that reflect the contents our inner mind. Once we stepped in, the mirrors surrounded us. Everywhere we looked, strange figures emerged from the mirrors, reflecting our hidden guilt and fear. Eventually, we disassociated from these disturbing images.

"Perception is a mirror, not a fact. And what I look on is my state of mind, reflected outward." (ACIM: W-304.1:3-4)

Welcome to the not-so-fun house called planet Earth. The ego has hidden our guilt and fear away from our conscious awareness. But it leaks into our awareness and we see unpleasant images all around us. We respond with fearful repulsion, not knowing it is our own distorted images that we have denied that are rising-up into our sphere of awareness. We do not recognize ourselves and the more we deride the images we see, the uglier they become. We feel defensive and victimized because everything we see is not as it should be, but we do not know it is of our own making at a quantum level.

> "Who but yourself evaluates a threat, decides escape is necessary, and sets up a series of defenses to reduce the threat that has been judged as real?... But afterwards, your plan requires that you must forget you made it, so it seems to be external to your own intent; a happening beyond your state of mind, an outcome with a real effect on you, instead of one effected by yourself. It is this quick forgetting of the part you play in making your 'reality' that makes defenses seem to be beyond your own control. But what you have forgot can be remembered, given willingness to reconsider the decision which is doubly shielded by oblivion." (ACIM: W-136.4:1—5:2)

Our 'decision' referenced in the last line refers to our decision to try to separate, then the cascading decisions associated with the first decision. We had a choice, to pursue the insane goal of specialness, or to answer the Loving Call of the Holy Spirit. In our dream-turned-nightmare, we made the decision to listen to, follow, and become identified with the ego. We made the decision to try to hide from our guilt in bodies in a seemingly separate world. We made the decision to deny our guilt-response for separating. Now in the not-so-fun house—planet Earth—this distorted world mirrors our own conflicted state of mind back to us.

"In your madness you overlook reality completely, and you see only your own split mind everywhere you look." (ACIM: T-13.V.6:5)

The Holy Spirit calls to us, waits for us, and is eager to help us leave the not-so-fun-house, but it can only work when we are ready to reconsider our decision to separate from God. This is the healing message of *A Course in Miracles.*

- "You whose mind is darkened by doubt and guilt, remember this: God gave the Holy Spirit to you, and gave Him the mission to remove all doubt and every trace of guilt that His dear Son has laid upon himself." (ACIM: T-13.XI.5:1)
- "To follow the Holy Spirit's guidance is to let yourself be absolved of guilt. It is the essence of the Atonement. It is the core of the curriculum." (ACIM: M-29.3:3-5)

Projection Casts Guilt and Fear Onto 'Others'

Our guilt and fear couldn't remain completely hidden in the unconscious mind. When shadows of unconscious guilt surfaced, it distressed us to the point that we wanted to escape the simulation. In order to keep us trapped and caught-up in the virtual reality, the ego devised another ploy to 'help' us avoid our feelings of guilt and fear—projection onto others.

There is only one Child of God, but our split-mind seemed to subdivide trillions of times over. The ego convinced us that the fragmented mind was now made up of separate consciousnesses, which were different than ourselves. The ego pointed at the fragments and called them 'others.' Then, as a solution for our intolerable guilt and fear, the ego taught us to deny and get rid of it by projecting it onto others.

In our current existence, our projections occur unconsciously, so all we know is we aren't haunted by our guilt, but we aren't aware that we passed it off to someone else. Then when we see it rise up in the external world, we do not recognize that it is *our own* projection coming back to us. This ego tactic is very convincing, and this insidious maneuver keeps us stuck in the illusion.

- "The ultimate purpose of projection is always to get rid of guilt." (ACIM: T-13.II.1:1)
- "Yet the one thing the ego never allows to reach awareness is that the special relationship is the acting out of vengeance on yourself." (ACIM: T-16.VII.5:3)

Sometimes the projection of guilt is turned onto ourselves. The guilt and fear is intolerable, so people may believe suicide will provide escape. Yet, even in death, we do not escape the guilt and fear. As described in Gary Renard's *Your Immortal Reality*, we are still haunted by our massive guilt complex after we leave the body.

> "ARTEN: …you can't break the cycle of birth and death and stop appearing to reincarnate as long as that unconscious guilt remains in the mind."

When our body dies, through suicide or natural causes, we still will not escape from the guilt and fear. We just cross over, regroup a bit, then reincarnate back into another body in an attempt to avoid the guilt and fear that we are haunted by, but don't understand. The vicious cycle of projecting our guilt onto others, then judging others when we see our darkness in them, repeats over and over again.

What the ego does not want us to know about its tactic of projections is, when we pass our guilt onto the 'other' person, we do not get rid of it. We just believe that we have, yet all we have done is add a layer to the debris field of our own unconscious guilt.

> "Perception is a mirror, not a fact. And what I look on is my state of mind, reflected outward. I would bless the world by looking on it through the eyes of Christ." (ACIM: W-304.1:3-5)

To fix the painful cycle of recycled guilt, we must go to the cause. When we look at the unconscious guilt as it arises, we don't feed into the ego's cyclic pattern.

> "It is not until beliefs are fixed that perceptions stabilize. In effect, then, what you believe, you do see." (ACIM: T-11.VI.1:3-4)

When we change our thought-system from the ego's system of separation to the Holy Spirit's wholeness thought system, by looking on the world through the eyes of Christ, everything changes. Our transformed thoughts of Oneness change our beliefs. When we change our belief, we change what we perceive.

> "From this place, where God and His Son dwell in peace and where you are welcome, you will look out in peace and behold the world truly. Yet to find the place, you must relinquish your investment in the world as you project it, allowing the Holy Spirit to extend the real world to you from the altar of God." (ACIM: T-12.III.10:8-9)

Blame 'Others' Who Behave Badly, Not Us

Whenever we see something happen in the world that we judge as 'bad,' that is actually our own guilt and fear that we wanted to get rid of through projection. However, the ego has successfully concealed this, so this concept is difficult to comprehend.

The ego programmed the holodeck to show us bad people doing bad things. As the ego encourages us to point out their bad behavior, we unilaterally judge and then blame 'others' for being bad. We are not consciously aware that the bad behavior or event we see outside of ourselves is our own unconscious guilt and fear projected onto someone else reflecting back to us. We believe we are the victim and 'they' did it. We have evidence and proof that they are bad, so we feel solidly justified in blaming them. It truly feels like we can escape our self-inflicted pain if we blame 'other' for what has gone wrong.

> "What you project you disown, and therefore do not believe is yours. You are excluding yourself by the very judgment that you are different from the one on whom you project. Since you have also judged against what you project, you continue to attack it because you continue to keep it separated. By doing this unconsciously, you try to keep the fact that you attacked yourself out of awareness, and thus imagine that you have made yourself safe." (ACIM: T-6. II.2:1-4)

It is remarkable how ingrained this projection tactic is. If we take time to be mindful of our thoughts, it may be astonishing how many of them automatically and systematically cast judgmental accusations of blame on our fellow companions! Even for one who tries to view the world with compassion and equanimity, it is easy to look askance at 'others' and devolve into the blame-game!

Imagine a dog chasing its tail. There is no 'other' dog. The dog just happens to notice that there is something following him which is rather unnerving. The dog cannot get away from the thing that is following him. "What's going on? Is it going to attack me? I'd better defend myself by attacking it first."

For the sake of the metaphor, imagine this example in a more extreme situation. The dog sees its tail and perceives it as 'other.' The dog doesn't like 'other' and he wants to make it stop coming after him. Biting his tail, the dog believes he has captured 'other' and he will make this suspicious character stop following him.

The dog bites down on his own tail, but suddenly there is pain. "Ow! That hurt! Why did the tail attack me?" Believing the tail was the cause of the pain, the dog bites down harder. More pain, more biting in response to the unprovoked attack by the tail.

In the extreme, the dog could end up at war with his own tail. Very ugly and painful things could happen to the tail, because it has been deemed 'other,' a malicious threat, causing great suffering to the dog.

As we unpack this metaphorical war, it seems obvious how ridiculous it is for a dog to make war with a part of itself. This is because we have a vantage point that easily shows the whole picture. It is more difficult to see that the exact same pattern applies to our own situation.

When we think we are blaming others for any reason, we

are blaming something that is a part of ourselves. There are no 'others.' It is not possible to be separate from anyone or anything, because everyone and everything is interconnected. Again, as quantum physics suggests, even at the level of form, we are all made up of the same energetic components, from the same unified field.

Judging and blaming 'others' is not helpful because our subconscious is aware that we are all interconnected. Imagine an island chain. Because we see the green land masses above the waterline, we believe they are individual islands. We truly believe that one island is here, another there, yet another over there; separate islands, each with its own fauna and flora. Yet, unseen below the waterline, there is land mass that connects all of the islands.

From the waterline, the islands appear to be individual. Yet drain all the water and we discover the interconnectedness of the island chain. They are the same. They are inextricably connected. There would be no above-water land mass without the interconnected below-water land mass.

This parallels the conscious and subconscious aspects of the mind. It is One Mind that appears to have trillions of separate islands. Yet, so the saying goes, "No man is an island." We can never blame 'others' without causing consequences to ourselves. When we blame 'others' for all the bad that 'they' did, our interconnected subconscious mind receives that input.

We believe we have cast blame away from ourselves, essentially getting rid of our guilt. But what we are not consciously aware of, is that our subconscious knows that we are connected to the 'others' we just blamed. Therefore, anything that we say or do or even *think* about other people, we are doing that to ourselves. It is unavoidable because below the 'waterline' of our consciousness, are the deep subconscious miracle impulses and the knowledge that we are all connected. We are connected to each other. We are all a part of each other. There is no separate island to blame and cast our guilt upon to get rid of it. It's all the same interconnected landmass.

There's a saying that encapsulates this message: "When we point our finger at someone else to cast blame, three fingers are pointing back at us." What makes understanding this difficult is that our guilt is hidden in our superficial subconscious, and we unconsciously project it outward. It genuinely seems we are separate from the other person who did something 'bad.' Many times, we cannot resist the temptation to use our 'evidence' of their guilt to emphatically prove that we have been wronged, that we are the victim here.

"If your brothers are part of you and you blame them
for your deprivation, you are blaming yourself."
(ACIM: T-11.IV.5:1)
We are each responsible for our own belief in blame, and conversely, the withdrawal of our blame from 'others.' I realize this can be a difficult concept to accept. The world we are experiencing is quite convincing to the contrary. Even if it is tempting to reject this concept, my recommendation is to lean into this one even further. Ask Spirit, Pause & Listen to see if a deeper understanding can come forward.

- "There is a very simple way to find the door to true forgiveness, and perceive it open wide in welcome. When you feel that you are tempted to accuse someone of sin in any form, do not allow your mind to dwell on what you think he did, for that is self-deception. Ask instead, 'Would I accuse myself of doing this?'" (ACIM: W-134.9:1-3)

- "As the ego would limit your perception of your brothers to the body, so would the Holy Spirit release your vision and let you see the Great Rays shining from them, so unlimited that they reach to God." (ACIM: T-15.IX.1:1)

Punish 'Them' Because 'They' Were Bad

In our dream of separation, not only have we tried to get rid of our guilt through projection onto 'others;' not only have we blamed 'others' and judged them to be 'bad;' we harbor a distorted belief that 'others' deserve to be punished for their wrong-doings, which are actually reflecting our own guilt and fear coming back to us like a boomerang.

If punishment is carried out, we sit back and relish it with pleasure. At the unconscious level, we believe we are vicariously relieved of our guilt as 'their' punishment seems to alleviate the need for God to punish us for separating, attacking God, and irrevocably tearing away a piece of Heaven.

- "Like to a dream of punishment, in which the dreamer is unconscious of what brought on the attack against himself, he sees himself attacked unjustly and by something not himself. He is the victim of this 'something else,' a thing outside himself, for which he has no reason to be held responsible." (ACIM: T-27.VII.1:3-4)
- "The ego's messages are always sent away from you, in the belief that for your message of attack and guilt,

will someone other than yourself suffer. And even if you suffer, yet someone else will suffer more." (ACIM: T-19.IV-B.15:1-2)

One of the many artificial constructs of this world that has never felt right to me is the concept of punishment. At the level of form, there is an apparent thirst for punishment in our society. This belief is embedded at every level, and there is so much inequity and injustice associated with it. When contemplating this societal expectation, it doesn't feel right, which is a tip-off that the ego has been up to no good.

What is punishment? What behaviors will be punished? What will the punishment consist of? How will the punishment be administered? Who gets punished and who doesn't? One person might be arrested, or even shot, for standing at a rally. Another person is permitted to commit the genocide of millions of people. Hmmm, that feels very incongruent.

Before learning of ACIM I remember telling my best friend, Kris, that I did not think the concept of punishment made sense. I referred to the concept of karmic debt, observing that it feels like a vicious cycle to me. I get the gist of it—if we feel the pain that we made another person feel, eventually we won't want to make anyone else feel that way. But this tit-for-tat system means that another person is obligated to harm us at some point. How does harm coming to us for something we did in the past, even in a past life, make this okay? What about that person's karma, after they have achieved retribution? One person causing another to suffer in order to seemingly settle the score feels wrong.

It seems that 'karmic debts' are never truly paid, only

recycled. We seem to be trapped in a dualistic system that advocates vengeance, harm and suffering. A futile cycle of unjust 'justice,' where our past mistakes hunt us down to exact revenge. And exactly how does one mete out the correct amount of suffering? When does this Hatfield and McCoy rivalry resolve? That dynamic feels an awful lot like the ego's scheme to keep us focused on judging the faults of others, and then demanding punishment of those who 'deserve' it.

Even at a personal level, most of us are 'keeping score,' maintaining our own little karmic tally of the people in our sphere of awareness. We are very much aware of the laundry list of insults and injuries that people have caused us. Maybe we would even like to see someone experience a downfall to give them a taste of their own medicine? This form of punishment is subtle, though just as insidious as a vicious feud.

> "'Vengeance is Mine, sayeth the Lord' is strictly a karmic viewpoint. It is a real misperception of truth, by which you assign your own 'evil' past to God. The 'evil conscience' from the past has nothing to do with God. He did not create it, and He does not maintain it. God does not believe in karmic retribution at all. His Divine Mind does not create that way. He does not hold the evil deeds of a person…against himself." (COA 3.III.5.1-7)

Rather than karmic retribution, there is a better way to resolve conflict, True Forgiveness, which embodies the Golden Rule. This is the ultimate key to our release. However, the ego does not want us to recognize this because that will be its undoing. While we view others as 'other' and project our guilt onto them; while we judge them and justify punishment for them, keep in mind that these accusations of guilt are reflecting our own hidden guilt. Anyone appearing to be outside of us is merely a distorted reflection of our separated self. This can be so difficult to conceptualize, but the sooner we learn this, the faster we will heal our mind.

> "The Golden Rule asks you to do unto others as you would have them do unto you…The Golden Rule is the rule for appropriate behavior. You cannot behave appropriately unless you perceive correctly. Since you and your neighbor are equal members of one family… You should look out from the perception of your own holiness to the holiness of others." (ACIM: T-1.III.6:2, 4-7)

The Golden Rule is a state of mind that envisions Perfect Truth, as *A Course in Miracles* explains, because we are all of the same Source. We are inextricably interconnected because there is One Child of God, whose mind seemingly splintered into many fragments. When someone seems to do something inappropriate, punishment is not ours to dictate.

> "Thus does the son of man become the Son of God. It is not really a change; it is a change of mind. Nothing external alters, but everything internal now reflects only the Love of God. God can no longer be feared, for the mind sees no cause for punishment." (ACIM: M-12.2:1-4)

CHAPTER 12

The Ego's Tactics that Keep Us Enmeshed in the Script

Threats of Disaster

Even though only the sleeping part of the mind believes it separated from God, that part *believes* the many convincing scenarios of separation. In the dream, the threat of scary events symbolizes our unconscious guilt and fear surfacing from the unconscious. Sometimes we experience looming fears from threatening circumstances beyond our control: cancer, diabetes, and viruses; war and nuclear attack; or earthquakes and rogue asteroids. These are still projections of our conflicted unconscious mind trying to rid ourselves of our guilt and fear of God's wrath. The ego projects this from our wrong-mind outward, onto external sources in the form of: The body malfunctioning or threats of man-made or natural disasters.

> "The world you see is a vengeful world, and everything in it is a symbol of vengeance. Each of your perceptions of 'external reality' is a pictorial representation of your own attack thoughts." (ACIM: W-23.3:1-2)

In December of 2020, during the Covid-19 pandemic, my mom had a mild stroke. At age 89, she had been remarkably healthy, but on that day she needed to go to the hospital. The first night she was there, the nurse told me I couldn't stay overnight because Covid policies didn't allow visitors to stay past 7:00pm.

Mom was definitely not herself; in her confusion, she was not making sense. When 7:00pm came, I did not want to go. I asked the nurses to let me stay, but they said it wasn't permitted. When I started to leave, my mom anxiously grasped at my hands with a surprisingly tight grip. I could barely remove myself from her bedside. I stopped at the nurse's station and said that Mom was agitated, and I was concerned she may be experiencing 'sundowners,' where patients become more confused in the evening and nighttime.

Feeling very doubtful about leaving, I asked the nurse to call me if Mom had any problems during the night no matter what time it was. I went home and made sure my cellphone sound was turned-up. There were no calls during the night, so I was hopeful that she had settled down after I left. Then I got a call from the nurse at 6:15am. I could hear Mom's nonsensical mutterings in the background. The nurse said that Mom had been hallucinating all night!

I was extremely disappointed that they did not call me as I had emphatically requested. When the nurse handed Mom the phone, she was so relieved to hear my voice because she believed that I was dead. Mom proceeded to relay all of the horrors that she had been through the night before. She was absolutely convinced that everything bad that could have happened, did happen. She believed that my husband and I had been murdered, as well as her beloved grandchildren. She was very distraught because her precious cat had been killed and her car set on fire. She said they took her to a room and injected her with the Covid virus. Even the doctor had been murdered. On and on she went, with absolute certainty, factually describing one horror after another. She had suffered with these atrocities all night long! Can you imagine believing that all those horrors actually happened?

I reassured her over and over, "Mom, none of that happened. I promise you, your mind was telling you stories. Mom, it's okay. We are safe. You are safe. Nothing bad happened." This helped a little, yet she was still pretty sure that it did happen. When I arrived at the hospital, we went over it again. She still could not believe that what she experienced that night was not true. She was there, how could it not have happened?

That evening, I appealed to the nurse to let me stay overnight with Mom. The nurse said they were actually planning to ask me to stay. Upon hearing this, I felt an upset brewing because my mom had suffered needlessly the night before. In my wrong-mind, there dwells an instinctual protective Mother Bear, and I was struggling to hold it at bay. Yet I knew this was my own unconscious guilt emerging through this experience. I Asked Spirit to help me see this situation differently. After Pausing & Listening, I sensed that her altered mental state caused her to slip into the layer of unconscious that houses our fears. It's as if the basement door was open and she took a step or two into the debris field of the unconscious. Then the thought came to mind that this was a very interesting lesson on the concept of our own hallucinations of events in this world. Having this insight helped me apply True Forgiveness to the situation.

"What if you recognized this world is an halluci-
nation? What if you really understood you made
it up? What if you realized that those who seem to
walk about in it, to sin and die, attack and murder
and destroy themselves, are wholly unreal?... Hallucinations disappear when they are recognized for
what they are. Believe them not and they are gone."
(ACIM: T-20.VIII.7:5—8:3)

Gradually, Mom came out her mental fog. Fortunately, now
that she's back to health, she doesn't remember much of that
experience.

The images and experiences of this world are very convincing. We, who believe we are in this world, have a terrible
time believing that the images and experiences of this world
are wholly unreal. However, the lesson of Mom's hallucinations helped me understand even more so what the summary
in the Introduction of the Course is talking about.

"Nothing real can be threatened. Nothing unreal exists. Herein lies the peace of God." (ACIM: T-in.2:2-4)

My mom's experience demonstrates how the mind can play
tricks on us, showing us misperceptions that cause us to
form incorrect beliefs. On the other hand, our habitual beliefs
can cause us to perceive incorrectly. When someone looks
through darkened glasses, everything they perceive through
the lenses will be dark.

When I was growing up, my father suffered from debil-
itating clinical depression and suicidal tendencies. He was a
dysfunctional genius—brilliant but overwhelmed by the belief in darkness everywhere. His mind was caught in a vicious
cycle of casting shadows of despair, then perceiving the world

as going to hell-in-a-handbasket. Over-focusing on the problems of the world, he ruminated on threats of nuclear attack, the Viet Nam war, and corrupt politicians.

At the level of form, he was not necessarily wrong about such problems, but he obsessed over them to the exclusion of all else. My father was highly sensitive and he dearly wanted to help humanity, but his anger masked his compassion. As a scientist, he saw evidence everywhere confirming his beliefs. As an engineer, he saw so many simple solutions to our problems. He was easily frustrated because he knew what would help, but no one listened. Then he would express his frustration with people in off-putting ways. What he did not realize is, at a quantum thought level, his rage against the injustice of it all was reinforcing the injustices he was perceiving.

Stuck in a cycle of self-fulfilling prophecy he made himself miserable, along with those around him. Growing up in this energy of angst, I heard and felt all those threats of doom-and-gloom that he dwelled upon. As a highly sensitive child, I absorbed his harsh criticisms of the world. I grew up living with high anxiety about nuclear annihilation, and other impending atrocities, believing that each day might be my last.

Finally, after surviving all those harrowing days and nights of looming disaster, I resolved that I was not going to buy into the threats of doom-and-gloom any more. I knew the world had its problems, but I began to realize that my father's lens was especially dark. Even though I did not know about the Course then, I believe that my intention of deliberately not following that dire ego-based thought pattern shifted my mental pattern to a healthier one. I knew there was a better way to live than constantly bemoaning all the ills of the world like a black hole of despair.

"I loose the world from all I thought it was." (ACIM: W-132)

Have you noticed society's attraction to 'threats of disaster' unfolding at any moment? We fixate on exaggerated threats of our demise probably more than we realize. Yet many of our fears of impending doom do not play out. We waste so much time worrying, it's virtually an addiction. From an ACIM perspective, all of our fears and frets are best handled by looking at them with the Holy Spirit at the very moment any of them arise in our mind—the relief from fear is so healing.

That is not to say that there isn't the potential for something like a civil war, a nuclear event or a natural disaster to unfold at this level of perception. Things could get very challenging if our dream of separation continues its nightmarish momentum because the separated mind has been seething with great conflict. Without a significant shift from conflict to healing, eventually, there could be an outward projection of this inner conflict.

"The history of humanity in the world as you see it has not been characterized by any genuine or comprehensive reawakening or rebirth. This is impossible as long as humanity projects in the spirit of miscreation." (COA 2.2.15.1-2)

Michael Sandler, who hosts *Inspire Nation,* a podcast and YouTube channel, used an interesting metaphor for this. He described a volcanic eruption as the outward expression of the inward conflict. Beforehand, surrounding areas experience rumblings and tremors, and smoke is seen emerging from the mountain. Then when the volcano erupts, molten lava can cause a great deal of destruction. Afterwards, with time, things settle down. As the lava cools, new land masses are formed. The event can be seen as traumatic, but growth can eventually be gleaned from the process. At this point in our perception, we may be experiencing some rumblings before an eruption of some kind.

Here is a suggestion for a more ACIM-aligned response to the ego's 'threats of doom.' No matter what appears to happen in the illusion, our Essence will not die from it. Yes, there may be some intense and scary times. We would prefer not to experience those challenging events, but if we continue to harbor conflict in our wrong-mind, then, it is possible that a corresponding conflict will eventually be expressed as an outward projection.

On the other hand, Michael Sandler's metaphor includes what happens after things settle from the volcanic eruption: growth, healing, and expansion. Numerous resources, including *The Disappearance of the Universe*, have indicated that there could be some type of deconstruction before the reconstruction. But the reprioritization and growth process will be healing and beneficial for the reconciliation of the split mind.

That is not to say that we should callously dismiss the apparent problems of the world. It is best to do what is practical at the level of form, while maintaining a deliberate awareness of the underlying ego-dynamic of the mind that projected those images. We can acknowledge that any disturbing experiences are not of God. It is just not possible, and therefore they simply cannot be true, even if we seem to be experiencing them —when an upset comes into our sphere of awareness, it is always a cue to Ask Spirit, Pause & Listen, applying True

Forgiveness as we are guided.

In our frightening dream, our conflicted wrong-mind has kept a death-grip on outdated thought patterns, which has generated incorrect beliefs, piling on more unconscious guilt and fear. There is a better way. Like a tidal wave building momentum, transformation is unfolding as we change our mind about the world. Maintaining awareness of our interconnectedness allows us to surf the crest of the wave as it glides-in to the shore. However, there are those who have fixated on the old paradigm. Those who try to stop the wave of change, will struggle more with the shifts as they unfold.

> "Change is always fearful to the separated, because
> they cannot conceive of it as a move towards healing
> the separation. They always perceive it as a move to-
> ward further separation, because the separation was
> their first experience of change." (ACIM: T-4.I.2:2-3)

In the face of threatened 'impending change,' there is healing work we can do within our minds, before, during and after these shifts occur. The most important thing we can do right now is to Ask Spirit for guidance, to practice True Forgiveness, and to connect with genuine Love to every being in the multiverse and beyond. I call it using our 'Mom-Goggles.' You know when we see young children through our Mom-Goggles (and even guys can use them), we see the adorable youngster as innocent and perfect and we just shower them with pure Love, naturally flowing from our heart. Similarly, it is helpful to wear those same adoring Mom-Goggles when viewing all Beings, as this Buddhist meditation from the Metta Sutta describes:

> *"Let us cultivate boundless goodwill.*
> *Let none deceive another or despise any being in any state.*
> *Let none in anger or ill-will wish another harm.*
> *Even as a mother watches over her child, so with bound-*
> *less Mind should one cherish all living beings, radiating*
> *friendliness over the whole world, above, below, and all*
> *around, without limit."*

This is not just a lofty and unattainable ideal, it is our Divine Calling. At the level of form, our collective consciousness has been losing ground in terms of our view of 'others.' Instead of cultivating a connection with all life-forms, our mindset has become much more polarized. Many of us have been looking askance at these 'others' as we encounter them in our sphere. Why? Because 'hell is distance from Oneness.' As we alienate ourselves farther away from our Oneness, we *feel* the fearful effects of even more alienation.

In this fearful state of self-isolation, we view other people as 'other.' Below our conscious awareness, from that unconscious layer, the ego prompts more division by projecting our own guilt and fear onto them. When we see our own ugliness in 'others,' we judge them as reprehensible and we are further repulsed. This pattern causes the collective unconscious to slip further into divisive inner conflict. The more intense the inner-conflict, the more intensive the outward projection will be.

> "Projection still has this 'hurling' connotation, because it involves hurling something you do not want, and regard as dangerous and frightening, to someone else. This is the opposite of the Golden Rule, and having placed this rule upside down, the reverse

of miracles, or projection, follows automatically."
(COA T-1.35.3:1-3)
The threat of 'mass devastation' is the ultimate projection 'hurling' the conflict of the inner-mind outward. What will we do with the ego's threats of impending doom? Take the bait? Feed the fear? Make it worse with hateful, polarizing rhetoric? Nope, we know that does not feel right at all. If we want to minimize the effects of a global outward projection, there is a better attitude to adopt.

Living the Golden Rule is the exact opposite of projection, both in theory and in application. Using our Mom-Goggles to practice treating All Beings compassionately, as we wish to be treated, is our Calling. Applying True Forgiveness universally, to every Being and every perceived event, is our True Function. The main message of the Course is to cultivate boundless goodwill by treating others not as 'other' but as our One Self; well and truly One-and-the-same. If you think about it, these are the same ideals exemplified by the one called Yeshua.

Living the Golden Rule takes time to develop, yet this practice will most assuredly lead to 'a better way' unfolding in our experience. As the better way unfolds, we will experience the Truth of this profound statement attributed to poet H. Hennenberg: "There is no 'I,' there is no 'you,' there is only WE."

As we each do our part to heal our mind with the Holy Spirit, we individually and collectively reduce the threat of experiencing the ego's 'disastrous effects.' Our willingness to heal our own mind now, facilitates the healing of the world before, during and after any perceived projection of the ego's disastrous scripts.

"Today, let us resolve together to accept the joyful tidings that disaster is not real and that reality is not disaster. Reality is safe and sure, and wholly kind to everyone and everything. There is no greater love than to accept this and be glad." (ACIM: T-16.II.8:5-7)

Distractions Keep Us Distracted

Within the dream world, we subsist in our bodies on this planet, struggling and striving, trying to survive until our bodies die. In the meantime, the ego plays out its separation scripts with seemingly endless parades of threats, traumas and dramas. These serve to distract us from asking WHY we are here and then discovering the Truth about God's All-Encompassing Love for us. For the ego knows that if we Ask, we will be answered.

"By becoming involved with tangential issues, it hopes to hide the real question and keep it out of mind. The ego's characteristic busyness with nonessentials is for precisely that purpose. Preoccupations with problems set up to be incapable of solution are favorite ego devices for impeding learning progress. In all these diversionary tactics, however, the one question that is never asked by those who pursue them is, 'What for?' This is the question that you must learn to ask in connection with everything." (ACIM: T-4.V.6:4-8)

A master illusionist distracts and draws attention away from the trickery unfolding onstage. While performing his act, the illusionist influences the audience with hypnotic suggestions, manipulating all the senses into a mesmerizing trance of acquiescence. The redirections are so subtle that audience members do not even realize they are being influenced. A master illusionist knows how to get into people's heads, diverting attention, then surprising the audience with something unexpected.

This sounds familiar—a remarkable description of the ego's tactics. A part of our mind became mesmerized by the tiny, mad idea of separation, which started as an innocent daydream. Then our attention was diverted and derailed, as the thought of separation went viral, turning the daydream into a nightmare.

It could be easily resolved with Spirit's help, but the ego's distracting maneuvers divert our attention away from this option. The ego, as master illusionist, uses elaborate devices to conceal its trickery. It influences our wrong-mind to believe the unbelievable.

- "Time is a trick, a sleight of hand, a vast illusion in which figures come and go as if by magic." (ACIM: W-158.4:1)
- "Complexity is nothing but a screen of smoke, which hides the very simple fact that no decision can be difficult." (ACIM: W-133.12:3)
- "The glass in which the ego seeks to see its face is dark indeed. How can it maintain the trick of its existence except with mirrors?" (ACIM: T-4.IV.1:6-7)

In the ego's scripted illusion, we believe we have no choice but to engage in the struggle to survive, yet eventually our bodies die anyway. Then we seem to return to do it all over again and again, ad infinitum. At any point in our devolving awareness, we could have asked the question that would help us return to Love. And we still can. What is that question? As stated in ACIM's Chapter 4, the question is, "What is this for?" This is the question that we must learn to Ask in connection with Everything!

This is why we Ask Spirit, Pause & Listen. The best way to Listen is to center ourselves in Peace. We are so accustomed to our busy-mind running in its hamster wheel, so very, very busy—but getting nowhere. How do we Listen? We simply step off the hamster wheel, and there we are within a moment of calm. In this still-point we can breathe and just be, and when we Ask, the answers naturally come to us.

- "The distractions of the ego may seem to interfere with your learning, but the ego has no power to distract you unless you give it the power to do so." (ACIM: T-8.I.2:1)
- "You are a mirror of truth, in which God Himself shines in perfect light. To the ego's dark glass you need but say, 'I will not look there because I know these images are not true.'" (ACIM: T-4.IV.9:1-2)

We Continually Seek Substitutions for God's Love

Even though we never lost God's all-encompassing Love, our fear of God became a barrier blocking our awareness of God's Love. Hiding inside the walls of our heart, in our wrong-mind, our little ego-self is so insecure and lonely, the thought of finding Love within that dark place seems impossible. Consequently, the ego directs us to search for security outside ourselves in the external world. Surely some thing, some body, or some place can provide the lasting Love and happiness we seek? Yet everything in the externally manifested world is impermanent, so any substitutions for God's Love will not last. There is no substitute for God's Love, and there is no need to seek outside ourselves to find it.

"Yet the ego, though encouraging the search for love very actively, makes one proviso; do not find it. Its dictates, then, can be summed up simply as: 'Seek and do not find.'" (ACIM: T-12.IV.1:3-4)

This drive to "Seek and do not find" is the central problem for nearly every one living in the space-time bubble. We have a compelling urge to seek for something to fill the void. It could be the drive to drive a certain kind of car really fast to make us feel more 'alive.' We may try consuming ever-greater amounts of food, drugs, or alcohol. Maybe more will finally satiate our insatiable appetite? Yet the aching emptiness remains. No amount of substance fills us up and keeps us permanently satisfied.

Even if we acquire many things, we can't take even one of them with us when we die. This brings me to an important insight I learned from an Episcopal minister way back in 2002. I was trying to articulate the futility of pursuing happiness through overeating, sex, drug addiction, adrenaline rushes, and the compulsion to acquire so many things—but I couldn't find the words. She then shared Blaise Pascal's perfect encapsulation of this insatiable urge to fill the void: "There is, in every human heart, a God-shaped hole that cannot be filled with any man-made thing, only that which is eternal could fill such an abyss."

That stopped me in my tracks. Yes! This 'God-shaped hole in every human heart' was a puzzle piece for my understanding of WHY we seek the world for some kind of lasting security. The hole in our heart cannot be filled with anything except Divine Love. I knew this, I knew it deep in my knowing Self, and finally it was expressed in words that made sense to me.

This prompted me to research Pascal's concept of the God-shaped hole in every human heart. There are many variations of the expression, and what follows is a compilation of various internet searches that express what I had been sensing, but could not articulate. 'The God-shaped hole in the human heart is, in fact, an infinite, terrifying abyss which I try to cover over with all sorts of false façades. But then a crack appears in the façade, and I see through it into the well of nothingness plunging down forever, and I hurl myself back in total horror. Only that which is eternal and completely transcendent could fill such an abyss.'

If it doesn't seem like we're afraid of the unconscious abyss of our fear of God, just think about the last time you were startled or fearful. Maybe it was looking down from a high ladder, or a close call in traffic, or being afraid of the dark. We may not seem to experience fear each waking moment, but under the surface is an unconscious layer of intense fear, ready to rise up at a moment's notice. Even relatively minor fears represent our deeply unconscious fear of God's torturous wrath. Remember, the ego projected our fear away from our awareness, into our unconscious mind, and then we forgot all about it.

We sense this abysmal chasm of guilt and fear, causing us to feel very insecure, so we try to pretend it isn't there. That doesn't work, so we reason that if we could just find something to fill the void, we would finally feel the comfort of lasting security. Spackle that crack in the façade! Yet each thing we set our hopes on doesn't do it. Even though it is futile, we keep searching for those substitutions to try to fill the void. Yet these impermanent things eventually break down and fail—like bodies and any thing man-made, or ego-made. And since the ego 'made' the multiverse, that would include any thing within the multiverse.

> "No one created by God can find joy in anything except the eternal; not because he is deprived of anything else, but because nothing else is worthy of him." (ACIM: T-8.VI.3:2)

We tried to substitute for God's Love, found out that was impossible, and we now Ask to be shown a better way. The Course shows us exactly how to find this better way, and that is to see the situation differently with Holy Spirit's guidance.

> "The Holy Spirit takes you gently by the hand, and retraces with you your mad journey outside yourself, leading you gently back to the truth and safety within. He brings all your insane projections and the wild substitutions that you have placed outside you to the truth. Thus He reverses the course of insanity and restores you to reason." (ACIM: T-18.I.8:3-5)

CHAPTER 13

The Atonement —
The Holy Spirit's Plan of Salvation

"The instant the idea of separation entered the mind of God's Son, in that same instant was God's Answer given. In time this happened very long ago. In reality it never happened at all." (ACIM: M-2.2:6-8)

THE HOLY SPIRIT **is the Still, Small Voice that Calls to Us from our Innermost Self**

"The Voice of the Holy Spirit is the Call to Atonement, or the restoration of the integrity of the mind." (ACIM: T-5.I.5:4)

When we listen to the Holy Spirit and follow our guidance, our illusions are gently dispelled and Truth is able to shine through to our mind. This is the meaning of that great phrase in the above quote, "the restoration of the integrity of the mind."

"The Holy Spirit's interpretation of fear does dispel it, for the awareness of truth cannot be denied. Thus does the Holy Spirit replace fear with love and translate error into truth." (ACIM: T-12.I.10:3-4)

Many people ask why God lets us suffer here. Some even decide there must not be a God, because there is so much suffering. However, the Course explains that our suffering is not generated by God, but by the part of our own mind that believes it is separate from God.

Once we realize that this world is an illusion that was 'made' by the separated mind, what do we immediately want? "Get me outta here, now!" And understandably so, however, it takes time to remove the defensive barriers that we placed around our mind in fear. ACIM explains that time is a learning device to hold the space for us as we learn to release ourselves from our self-imposed imprisonment.

We may ask, "But why can't it just be all gone? Why won't God just take me Home now?" The primary reason is that we are not ready to let go of our defensive barriers because we believe they provide us with security. If we aren't ready to let them go, it feels scary to have those layers lifted.

> "Defenses, like everything you made, must be gently turned to your own good, translated by the Holy Spirit from means of self-destruction to means of preservation and release." (ACIM: T-14.VII.5:8)

Listening to the still, small Voice of the Holy Spirit within our right-mind is the key to allowing our defensive barriers to be transformed to messages of Perfect Love. We cannot pay attention to Spirit's Voice of guidance if we do not Pause and take time to step away from the distractions of the world.

> "Be not afraid today to circumvent the voices of the world. Walk lightly past their meaningless persuasion. Hear them not. Be still today and listen to the truth." (ACIM: W-106.3:1-4)

Before we can return to our True Home, we have deep-seated false perceptions stuck in our unconscious mind that need to be gradually shifted into true perceptions. When we Pause & Listen, it is much easier to realize we have been imprisoned by our own dualistic beliefs.

> "His Voice awaits your silence, for His Word can not be heard until your mind is quiet for a while, and meaningless desires have been stilled." (ACIM: W-125.6:2)

Once we Pause and become still, and Listen to Spirit's guidance, we will know what is ready to be looked at and Truly Forgiven with Spirit. Eventually, you may notice that the practice of Asking Spirit, Pausing & Listening allows what was once the 'still, small Voice' of the Holy Spirit in our mind to become more prominent and easier to hear.

> "Let my own feeble voice be still, and let me hear the mighty Voice for Truth Itself assure me that I am God's perfect Son." (ACIM: W-118.2:2)

True Forgiveness is our Function and Purpose

We want to be saved from our miserable dream, but if we don't understand how to accomplish this, we will remain captive to its effects. A concept that is not well-understood is that even when our bodies die, we don't escape the ego's dualistic trap because our unconscious guilt and fear keeps us stuck in a futile cycle of birth and death.

Gary Renard's second book *Your Immortal Reality* explains that when our bodies die here, we often seem to transition to a better place that is thought to be Heaven because it seems so much better than this hell-on-Earth. Conversely, sometimes people's unconscious guilt is overwhelming, so they imagine themselves to be in a place of hellish torment. However, *Your*

Immortal Reality explains that both types of these between-life experiences are also part of the dualistic illusion.

> "Such is each life; a seeming interval from birth to death and on to life again, a repetition of an instant gone by long ago that cannot be relived. And all of time is but the mad belief that what is over is still here and now." (ACIM: T-26.V.13:3-4)

The between-life experience may be wonderful for a while, but as this quote explains, the death of our body does not free us from our unconscious guilt and fear of God that began with original belief in separation. Eventually, we are so intensely plagued by our guilt and fear that we are compelled to leave the between-life realm in hopes of escaping it. We dream up another body and we continue the futile cycle of birth and death. However, all of those experiences of between-life, birth, life and death are just the cyclical dreams of the seemingly separated mind.

> "The body's serial adventures, from the time of birth to dying are the theme of every dream the world has ever had." (ACIM: T-27.VIII.3:1)

It may be disturbing to consider that the continual struggle to live on this planet, and the inevitability of bodily death, will just end up repeating over and over again. That seems pretty depressing, but the Course offers True Forgiveness as the way out, rather than the futile cycle of constantly trying to evade our unconscious guilt and fear. The only genuine release is to heal our mind of its false belief that it separated, and to let Spirit clear away the guilt and fear hidden in our unconscious.

This does not mean that each and every incident that ever seemed to occur in time since the OOPS needs to be forgiven. It is more a matter of releasing patterns and their related effects which the Holy Spirit will adjust as we recognize the pattern. This is a process of allowing Spirit to dispel each layer of our unconscious guilt and fear until eventually all the debris of guilt and fear has been cleared away through True Forgiveness. As explained in *Your Immortal Reality*:

> "PURSAH: When your forgiveness lessons are complete, then not one trace of guilt will remain in your unconscious mind. At that point, you will break the cycle of birth and death, and never dream of going into a body again. That is the end of reincarnation…. (keep forgiving) whatever comes up in front of your face. That's the work of salvation, and it's the most important thing that anyone can ever do for themselves."

If we want to exit this strange world of perceived separation, releasing our unconscious guilt and fear through True Forgiveness is our true function and purpose.

Allowing the nightmare of separation to be replaced by a gentle dream of peace

> "You do not remember how to look within for you do not believe your home is there. Yet the Holy Spirit remembers it for you, and He will guide you to your home because that is His mission." (ACIM: T-12.IV.5:4-5)

We have been so confused by our nightmare of separation that if we suddenly awakened we would be terrified, believing we would need to defend ourselves from God's awe-inspiring Presence. It is better that our return to Love is a gradual dawning in our awareness, rather than an abrupt shift.

We are more attached to our illusions than we may re-alize. As an example, recall something from your past that made you angry, sad, or fearful. Bring the details and emo-tions of the event into your awareness. Next, go ahead and just let memory that go. Just release it—Don't hold onto that deep-seated emotion any more…Well?….That is not such an easy thing to do. If we aren't ready to let it go, chances are the thought of letting go makes us want to clutch our story that much more tightly. Even if we want to let it go, it is not as easy as it sounds to just 'get over it.'

These layers of collected experiences seem to make up our identity. If we don't reconsider our stories with Spirit's guidance, letting go of even one of our cherished narratives is not easy. We came up with one memory as an example, but there are thousands of memory patterns that we've collected and hoarded over our lifetimes.

A scene from the movie *Labyrinth*, released in 1986, dem-onstrates this point. Sarah, the main character, is stuck in a labyrinth, which is a symbolic representation of the uncon-scious mind. In her journey, she encounters many characters. At one point, she meets people who are carrying enormous collections of seemingly useless items, all tethered in a huge bundle on their backs. Their burdens are cumbersome and they look ridiculous trying to get around with their bulbous baggage constantly getting in the way. However, trying to re-move just one item from of that pile of junk would lead to fierce defense, as if it was their most prized possession.

Our own 'hoarded junk' consists of our unconscious emotional baggage that is carried with us everywhere we go. It's difficult for us to remove, and we don't even know how to reach most of it. However, the Holy Spirit has the ability to help us release each layer. But only when we are ready to see our prized possessions, our fearful stories of woe and deprivation, differently. Are they valuable or useless? Are they truly helpful, or does bearing our baggage make us weary? How does it serve us? How, indeed? Let the Holy Spirit help us sort this baggage out!

[Note: Just as I was writing this, a roach crawled onto the screen of my laptop and I quickly put the laptop on the coffee table and stepped away. The fascinating thing about the timing of that event is, I've got emotional baggage associated with roaches. My 'hoarded story of woe' goes like this: When I was seven we moved into a house, that, unbeknownst to us, was roach-infested. It took many attempts to eradicate them. This happened in the 1970's exactly when a movie called *The Bug* was released. The movie trailers depicted people being attacked by roaches, which triggered nightmares and extreme anxiety in me. I was unable to filter these experiences and I developed a lingering phobia of roaches.

This unexpected visitation from a wood roach, however, didn't make me go catatonic as it would have years ago. Fortunately, I've already done True Forgiveness work on this and have made great strides, but the unexpected trigger informs me there are remnants that I am ready to release. The timing of this event was interesting considering I was writing about letting go of emotional baggage, then one of my own deep-seated triggers creeps into my sphere of awareness. As I stepped away from my laptop, I immediately Asked Spirit, Paused & Listened for help and then Lesson 31, "I am not the victim of the world I see," came to mind.

I allowed my residual feelings of roach revulsion to sur-face—the childhood nightmares and disturbing memories. As I affirmed that "I am not the victim of the world I see," I felt a shift, an unlocking that felt significant—a miracle. Every time I give my lingering fears and bad memories to Spirit, I'm filled with so much peace and I can feel myself shifting to a gentler dream.]

This is an example of how Spirit knows the whole plan that releases all of us from our collective nightmare—and the unfolding plan is deliberate and well-timed. As long as we are willing to use True Forgiveness, Spirit can help unlock the interlocking chain of forgiveness in perfect sequence.

> "Miracles are part of an interlocking chain of for-giveness which, when completed, is the Atonement. Atonement works all the time and in all the dimen-sions of time." (ACIM: T-1.I.25:1-2)

It may seem that no progress is being made as layers of guilt and fear are removed, however, as we continue the process, we will feel the benefits. After working through some layers, ACIM students often feel much more at peace in their lives. It's good to be aware, however, that sometimes there can be phases of unsettling with many shifts occurring. Yet as we take each concern to Spirit, eventually they resolve, which re-sults in an even more peaceful state of mind.

This gentle undoing process is part of the Holy Spirit's plan to help us relinquish our nightmare. Spirit undoes the con-flicted aspects of our bad dream, then right perceptions take their place. As we build complete trust that Spirit will handle every concern that arises, our nightmare is gently transformed into a serene dream of peace.

"Rest in the Holy Spirit, and allow His gentle dreams to take the place of those you dreamed in terror and in fear of death. He brings forgiving dreams, in which the choice is not who is the murderer and who shall be the victim. In the dreams He brings there is no murder and there is no death." (ACIM: T-27.VII.14:3-5)

Once the fragments of our Christ Mind join as One, God takes the final step of salvation

"Here you are led, that God Himself can take the final step unhindered, for here does nothing interfere with love, letting it be itself." (ACIM: T-18.IX.10:4)

The Golden Rule tells us love your neighbor as yourself—to treat every being as you wish to be treated. The Course embodies the Golden Rule at the deepest level. We learn to treat every being as we wish to be treated because we *are* that Being. We Love all equally because we recognize our Oneness in All.

True Forgiveness is the modality that helps us heal all of our misperceptions so that our mind is able to perceive the truth of Oneness throughout creation. This is not the 'unicorns farting rainbows, everything is wonderful because everything is love' that we pretend to believe. That doesn't undo the burden of unconscious guilt and fear that holds our mind stuck in a futile cycle of birth and death. We must do the work of taking our guilt and fear to Spirit that it may be released because we see that each manifested belief in separation is not true and never was. We cannot return to Love until we accept the healing of our mind.

While we believe our mind is fractured into many selves,

we simply cannot enter our ultimate reality of Oneness. This is not because we are in trouble, it is because it is impossible to understand Oneness if we are not at One with each other. Twoness cannot know Oneness. As long as we see differences and contrasts in others, we cannot enter into our True Home because our True Essence has no differences or contrasts.

As long as we think we are above some people and below others, we cannot return to our awareness of everyone's equal Perfection. We must first release our false images of disparity to see the ultimate equality that is. Everything in Essence is the same—there can be nothing that is not the same —that is what Essence means. We literally cannot perceive the wholeness of it if we are seeing something that appears to be better or worse, higher or lower, uglier or more beautiful.

> "To you and your brother is given the power of salvation, that escape from darkness into light be yours to share; that you may see as one what never has been separate, nor apart from all God's Love as given equally." (ACIM: T-25.II.11:5)

If we look at another person and believe they are 'other,' if we judge them as bad and deserving of punishment, so we will see ourselves, because it is our own shadow we see in them. While interposing that division between us, we simply will not be able to accept a unified reality.

If we wish to return to our True Home, we have to see the rest of the beings of the world in a new Light, by working with Spirit through every single pattern of remaining debris within our unconscious mind. Every judgment-pattern, transformed into Light. Every upset-pattern looked at with Spirit. Every grievance-pattern gracefully released in peace.

Every person's innocence revealed through the True Vision of Christ's Vision.

While we decline to participate in this transformative work, we remain stuck, going round and round, yet getting nowhere. And so it will remain, until the pure intention to see all fragments of the One Child of God as One is genuine. Then finally, the ultimate Golden Rule 'See your neighbor as One with you' is realized in the One Mind. The Light of Truth unfolds across the world like a soft blanket gently floating down, bringing us together and connecting All the separated ones.

> "The light that joins you and your brother shines throughout the universe, and because it joins you and him, so it makes you and him one with your Creator."
> (ACIM: T-22.VI.15:1)

When we all are joined together as One Child of God, we will be at complete peace within the gentle dream. When we are entirely without guilt or fear, God is then able to take the final step, returning our awareness to our perfect state of Oneness together—Together Is Home.

> "Today we ask of God the gift He has most carefully preserved within our hearts, waiting to be acknowledged. This the gift by which God leans to us and lifts us up, taking salvation's final step Himself."
> (ACIM: W-168.3:1-2)

CHAPTER 14

Miracle Methods—True Forgiveness Practices

ONE OF the most important redefined religious concepts in the Course is Forgiveness. In the typical practice of forgiveness, someone does something hurtful to me, causing me to hold a grievance against that person. After a while, I may decide to 'forgive' them for what they did to me. But what does that 'forgiveness' look like?

Sometimes I say I forgive them, yet only under certain conditions; maybe I expect an apology or restitution. Or I might say I have forgiven, but I hold onto the grievance, bringing up the same complaint again later. Sometimes I'll say I'm 'forgiving' them because that makes me the bigger person. Yet do these tactics really embody True Forgiveness? In *A Course in Miracles*, these are the ego's conditional and dualistic forms of 'forgiveness' known as 'forgiveness-to-destroy.' [Note: The Song of Prayer, Section 2: Forgiveness, explains forgiveness-to-destroy quite nicely.] The Course explains that this is not True Forgiveness because it reinforces the belief that God's One Son can be separate and harmful to itself.

ACIM's True Forgiveness methods correct the cause of our grievance by transforming our incorrect belief, which releases our unconscious guilt and fear. This is key because, even though the Old Original Perceived Separation never happened, we *believe* it did, and it is this false belief that is in need of healing. To heal our unconscious guilt and fear about the OOPS, we do not need to try to go back to the point of the OOPS when time began and try to forgive it. We heal our false belief in the original separation by paying close attention to anything that comes up into our current awareness that upsets our peace of mind.

Within the space-time bubble of perception, the ego invents endless scripts depicting scenarios of separation; the upset could be a memory, an interaction with someone, or a worry about a future event. It doesn't matter what the scenario is, the Holy Spirit has the antidote that dispels every single aspect of the ego's scripts. All we need do is Ask Spirit, Pause & Listen for help.

It's lovely to know that we have the option to significantly abbreviate our self-imposed 'life sentence' here through the use of miracles. However, as students of *A Course in Miracles* learn of this amazing tool, one particular question arises: *What the heck is a miracle?*

As with other traditional biblical terms, ACIM expands the meaning of the word 'miracle.' The typical connotation we associate with a miracle is an unusual event involving heroics, statistical improbabilities, and physical impossibilities—a mother lifts a car to save her child, or a person pronounced dead revives after a seemingly impossible period of time. Such miracles tend to be the exception, not the norm.

In True Forgiveness terms, the meaning is significantly different, and we have the potential to activate multiple miracles throughout the day. Even though the Course offers numerous descriptions of what a miracle is, for a long time I still felt unsure of what it truly meant. When I began to experience miracles, a deeper understanding came to me. Now I think of an ACIM miracle as a paradigm shift where Love replaces fear in our mind, moving us farther along our learning path.

> "Every chance given him to heal is another opportunity to replace darkness with light and fear with love." (ACIM: T-14.III.6:2)

This is what is so nifty about the miracle, when we truly forgive a present upset. Once we realize the upset was based on a false belief, the Holy Spirit adjusts the timeline of both the past and future.

> "It must be understood, however, that whenever you offer a miracle to another, you are shortening the suffering of both of you. This corrects retroactively as well as progressively." (ACIM: T-2.V.10:7-8)

This means that any patterns that are released in the present are undone throughout the entire space-time continuum.

> "(Miracles) undo the past in the present, and thus release the future." (ACIM: T-1.I.13:3)

As I understand it, within the space-time bubble timeline, without the use of miracles, all the separated minds do eventually accept that the separation never occurred; then we all reunite, merging into Oneness. However, in terms of linear time, this will take eons upon eons. In addition, within the timeline, a great deal of suffering is experienced along the way. The Holy Spirit's plan of salvation is awaiting our willingness to shorten that arduous pathway in time. This is where the miracle comes in.

"For what would seem to need a thousand years can easily be done in just one instant by the grace of God." (ACIM: W-196.4:5)

Metaphorically, I think of it in terms of the board game Candyland. The Gingerbread game pieces are placed at the starting point and they follow a convoluted pathway leading to 'Home Sweet Home.' On the original gameboard, there are bridges along the pathway — the Rainbow Trail and Gumdrop Pass. If we land on the right spot, we can cross the bridge and avoid a section of the pathway. We end up much further along in the journey Home and we avoid certain pitfalls along the way.

When this metaphor first came to me, I shared it with my best friend Kris. The very next day, I opened a cabinet door that was high up—we had moved into the house about six months beforehand, so I just hadn't looked in that high cabinet yet—well, what did I see staring back at me but two Candyland game pieces, one red and one green, just sitting there in the empty cabinet! I have to say, I am not often rendered speechless, but that in that moment of confirmation, I was profoundly stunned. Doesn't Spirit have a delightful sense of humor?

In applying the miracle to our lives, we can Ask Spirit to be our bridge, shortening our journey to 'Home Sweet Home,' thus saving time and avoiding unnecessary suffering. The miracle as a bridge not only shortens the pathway, but erases previous, as well as unused, pathways that are no longer needed. That part of the ego's script, and all its related ramifications disappear, being erased from the mind that made them up.

"You do not have to continue to believe what is not true unless you choose to do so. All that can literally disappear in the twinkling of an eye because it is merely a misperception." (ACIM: T-2.I.3:3-4)

Before we explore the Basic True Forgiveness Steps, it is important to understand why miracles are integral to the True Forgiveness process. As mentioned in previous chapters, we are not aware of the enormous guilt complex that lies just beneath our conscious awareness. Remember that unconscious conglomeration of guilt and fear we made up because we believe we separated from God? The way that we heal from this unseen seething abscess, is to deliberately and resolutely hold the following insights within our conscious awareness.

1. **Understand why the OOPS seemed to happen, recognize that a fearful guilt complex seemed to arise from the OOPS, and acknowledge we have hidden it in our unconscious mind.**

In the ultimate reality, we are One with everything that is Perfect Love. The illusion of space-time began when we had a tiny insane thought that caused us to believe we were separated from God. In reaction to our erroneous belief that we are separate, we felt horribly guilty and intolerably fearful of God. The ego coerced us to hide from God, and then it hid our guilt and fear from ourselves by denying it, sending it into our unconscious mind. These unconscious beliefs in guilt and fear keep us stuck in the ego's space-time bubble.

"These mad beliefs can gain unconscious hold of great intensity, and grip the mind with terror and anxiety so strong that it will not relinquish its ideas about its own (need for) protection." (ACIM: W-138.8:1)

2. **Everything we seem to see outside of us, including events and the behavior of others, is our own unconscious guilt and fear projected outward.**

We have blocked the Light of Truth in our mind. These layered barriers project the shadows of our own darkness onto our brothers. Not knowing it is our own shadow, we judge the darkness in our brothers and declare *them* to be sinful. We then blame them and demand that they be punished for their sins.

> "My sinless brother is my guide to peace. My sinful brother is my guide to pain. And which I choose to see, I will behold." (ACIM: W-351)

3. **The Holy Spirit helps us Truly Forgive our unconsciously held false beliefs about ourselves and others.**

As we live day to day in the world, our function is to allow Spirit to remove the blocks of darkness from our own unconscious mind, dispelling the darkness we saw in our brother. This is True Forgiveness.

> "Praying for others, if rightly understood, becomes a means for lifting your projections of guilt from your brother, and enabling you to recognize it is not he who is hurting you. The poisonous thought that he is your enemy, your evil counterpart, your nemesis, must be relinquished before you can be saved from guilt." (ACIM: S-1.III.1:4-5)

4. **The miracle is the means to transform our guilt and fear, allowing the Light of Truth to shine into our mind.**

- "In silence, close your eyes upon the world that does not understand forgiveness, and seek sanctuary in the quiet place where thoughts are changed and false beliefs laid by." (ACIM: W-126.10:1)

- "The light of guiltlessness shines guilt away because, when they are brought together, the truth of one must make the falsity of its opposite perfectly clear." (ACIM: T-14.VI.4:2)

5. **As we no longer cherish our false beliefs, the barriers we used to hide and defend ourselves from God are gently undone by the Holy Spirit.**

- "There is no barrier between God and His Son, nor can His Son be separated from Himself except in illusions." (ACIM: T-18.VI.9:3)

- "The Holy Spirit atones in all of us by undoing, and thus lifts the burden you have placed in your mind." (ACIM: T-5.IV.6:1)

6. **For each barrier that is lifted, we advance on the timeline that returns our awareness to Home Sweet Home.** "The miracle thus has the unique property of abolishing time to the extent that it renders the interval of time it spans unnecessary." (ACIM: T-1.II.6:5)

7. **Together Is Home**
"To Him we go together. Take your brother's hand, for this is not a way we walk alone. In him I walk with you, and you with me. Our Father wills His Son be one with Him." (ACIM: W-rV.in.9:5-8)

Every word in this book has been leading up to the expression of those seven key concepts of the Course. I believe they are the most important insights I have learned in my entire life, and all lifetimes that have gone before. I try to remain keenly aware of them as I follow my learning path within the space-time bubble. Being anchored by these foundational insights, motivates me to practice True Forgiveness as often as the prompt arises. Whenever I notice that an ego-based reaction is coming up in my mind, I do not repress it, I bring it to the table. I acknowledge that it is alerting me to the need to release a layer of my own guilt and fear by practicing True Forgiveness.

It might be surprising to learn that these kinds of miracles actually can occur anywhere for anyone. I experienced this type of miracle before I knew what they were. They occurred when my mind was receptive to re-thinking, but this only occurred randomly, when I happened to stumble across the right frame of mind. The Basic True Forgiveness Steps enable us to consistently utilize miracles whenever we feel guided to do so. When we understand why miracles are needed, what they can do, and how to use them, we are enormously empowered to heal the unhealed unconscious mind. These steps employ an extremely reliable thought system that allows miracles to unfold at any time. The following is an outline of the Basic True Forgiveness Steps that anyone can use for any circumstance.

1. **Notice the upset** — Notice whenever something upsets our peace of mind. In the past, we would hope to avoid those feelings, memories and experiences. Not anymore! Now we say, "Oh boy, here comes another True Forgiveness opportunity!" Then we immediately Ask Spirit, Pause & Listen for help.

2. **Notice ego-based patterns** — Identify our feelings and beliefs associated with the person or event that has triggered a reaction in us—taking notes is helpful.

* Ask "What am I feeling? Do I feel it showing up in my body somewhere? What does it remind me of? What is the pattern?"

* Ask "What are my beliefs about this situation? What evidence and behaviors am I seeing with the body's eyes?"

* As the feelings and beliefs are identified, look at the overall pattern. Then see that this is an ego-based pattern. Once the ego-based pattern is identified, reflect on how the situation or the other person's pattern is mirroring *our own* pattern. (This can be tricky, because it can be very difficult to believe it is our own pattern. It may be tempting to think, 'They are doing this, not me. What's more, they are doing this *to* me.' It is helpful to Ask Spirit, Pause & Listen to this part in particular to let the pattern-recognition come up into your mind.)

* Once we see our own ego-based pattern, take a second to imagine how that ego-based reaction first emerged

during the Old Original Perceived Separation. Then we recognize that we have been allowing the pattern to keep repeating since the OOPS.

3. **Choose Again — Choose Spirit** — We acknowledge that we have been using our wrong-mind. As we choose again, we declare we want to think with our right-mind and we want to be Spirit-led.

4. **Ask Spirit, Pause & Listen** — We Ask Spirit to look at our feelings and beliefs with us. Then we Pause & Listen for a message of Truth to emerge.

As we look at the problem with Spirit, we are able to see the Truth in our right-mind, through Christ's Vision. [Note: Sometimes the message comes through later when we aren't focused on it. We don't want to force it, so it's helpful to remember this mantra: Don't force it, don't block it, allow it to flow naturally.]

As we allow Spirit to communicate this new perspective into our awareness, we can release our false beliefs because we now know they are useless and do not serve us. Our mind naturally shifts from upset to Peace, then from Peace to Love. It may be instantaneous, or it may unfold gradually with time, but as long as we are ready to change our mind, a shift will occur.

5. **Spirit Adjusts intervals of Time** — We affirm that we are willing to let Spirit undo all the consequences of our error throughout the space-time continuum. This step occurs naturally, but it can feel even more freeing to affirm

that we would like for Spirit to do this.

To review, here is the streamlined version of the Basic True Forgiveness Steps:

1. **Notice the upset** — see it as an opportunity to Truly Forgive, Ask Spirit for help.
2. **Notice our ego-based patterns** — acknowledge the feelings and beliefs, understand that it is our own ego-based reaction projected outward, and relate it to the repeating pattern of the OOPS.
3. **Choose again, choose Spirit** — Realize we've been using our wrong-mind and actively choose to think with our right-mind.
4. **Ask Spirit, Pause & Listen** — Give our feelings and beliefs to Spirit, look at them with Spirit, and Ask to see them differently. Pause & Listen for a healing message.
5. **Spirit adjusts intervals of time** — Though Spirit takes care of this for us, I like to affirm my gladness for this releasing process.

"The miracle substitutes for learning that might have taken thousands of years. It does so by the underlying recognition of perfect equality of giver and receiver on which the miracle rests. The miracle shortens time by collapsing it, thus eliminating certain intervals within it." (ACIM: T-1.II.6:7-9)

What I didn't comprehend for a long time is that the shift of the miracle is effortless on our part. I was willing to work on forgiveness, but I would struggle and strive to forgive a person or situation, or myself. When I was actively trying to forgive the situation, I was combining the world's dualistic forgiveness approach with ACIM's True Forgiveness, and it was just not as effective because the more I tried to let go, the more I held on to it.

When I say that the shift is effortless, that is not to say that every aspect of True Forgiveness is effortless. When a forgiveness opportunity arises, uncomfortable emotions can trigger deeply unsettling feelings. When I experience this it feels like trying to steer a vehicle through a sharp corner. As I'm getting carried away with my emotions, I feel the heavy inertia pulling me sideways. It's as if I'm teetering on the edge of a steep ravine—the slippery slope of emotional defense. It takes determination to stay on course. However, even if I end up losing control for a time, I can forgive that too. No matter how far we drift off course, we can always get back on track with Spirit's help and continue to move forward on our learning path.

Though we don't have to use the Basic True Forgiveness Steps for True Forgiveness to be effective, I find that they help me recognize the ego set-up and my reaction patterns. This gives me perspective on why the ego's plan was an epic fail, that there is a better way, and that I choose that better way. Within the five steps that I now use, I have found the following features to be absolute game-changers for my own personal True Forgiveness practice.

My feelings & beliefs associated with the trigger — Some Course teachers say not to let the ego get a boost out of bringing up all the guilt and emotions. I have found it helpful to feel into the trigger and dredge up the muck that was lurking below in the unconscious, as long as we don't cause harm to ourselves and others. We are safe with Spirit, and it can be enlightening to recognize the depth of the emotional beliefs that have been influencing us. The emotions have been suppressed for so long, I wouldn't want to miss out on dispelling them by continuing to hold them back. I love Course teacher David Hoffmeister's saying, "Cough it up and spit it out. All of it. Get it all out."

Relate the ego patterns to the OOPS — Since True Forgiveness is retroactive, it is not absolutely necessary to connect the dots back to the OOPS when practicing the True Forgiveness Steps. However, in my own experience, the key has been seeing the ego patterns from the current issue symbolizing the repeating ego patterns that have continued to play out since the OOPS. This is not to try to actually remember it, but to think how it must have felt at the time of the OOPS.

For example, if feelings of anxiety are coming up, take a moment to reflect on our anxiety from the isolation we experienced during the OOPS. If we feel wounded, imagine how wounded we felt when we thought God abandoned us. If we currently feel regretful, think of the hopeless regret we felt when we believed we ruined our state of Perfect Oneness. These are snapshot insights, not dragged out self-flagellations.

I find this effective because it helps me step back from my attachment to the current situation. Declaring that this is just an old recycled pattern symbolizing the OOPS lets the air out of my blustering ego-trip I was getting carried away with.

Recognize the trigger is our own pattern — No matter what the other person seemed to do, that is not relevant to our inward True Forgiveness process. It only served to show us our own unhealthy pattern which represents a layer of our own guilt and fear that is ready to be released.

This is a subtle yet highly significant insight. True Forgiveness addresses our own pattern of unconscious feelings and beliefs. The reason we are experiencing the current set of upsetting factors is for the sole purpose of bringing up a barrier that was hidden in our unconscious mind. The current situation is just a vehicle that is delivering an aspect of our forgotten guilt and fear onto the doorstep of our conscious awareness. It is not about what someone else did to us, or about something that happened to us.

It may be difficult to accept this, because the events seem so real and convincing. But in this virtual reality, the sooner we grasp the bigger picture of why there seems to be an upset happening, the sooner we will know how to work with it and get past it, propelling ourselves along our learning pathway. For me, being aware of the bigger picture makes it much easier to change my mind about the current situation.

Ask Spirit, Pause & Listen — When we Ask Spirit to help us see this differently, we Pause & Listen to let Spirit's answer come into our awareness and we receive an insight that is specific to the situation. I had not picked-up on that nuance before. In this step-by-step True Forgiveness progression, the Ask, Pause & Listen is essential for Spirit's answer to come through; we are not the ones deciding what the healing message is, we are allowing it to arise in our mind.

Imagine that a message is being sent to us in Morse Code. It is essential to pause and listen to the dots and dashes that are sent over the communication line or the message will be missed. Likewise, by Asking Spirit, we open the lines of communication, then we Pause & Listen to allow the communication from Spirit to come through into our right-mind.

The healing message may arrive immediately, or it may surface a bit later. Once we receive Spirit's profound insight, it will be far greater than what we would have come up with on our own. The Pause & Listen is the pivot-point where the Holy Spirit shows us that what we thought was real and harmful is false and empty, exactly like the Old Original Perceived Separation which seemed devastatingly harmful, but it was truly nothing at all.

Seeing this, we naturally have a change of heart. What seemed so justified, now seems quite ridiculous, and we want to move forward in Peace without that burdensome baggage. Then Spirit collapses the related learning pathways that no longer need to be experienced. That golden moment of being ready to question our beliefs and to change our mind becomes the Holy Instant, the healing opportunity the Holy Spirit has been waiting for!

> "And look an instant, (on your illusions that) you left behind at last and finally passed by. This was the ego — all the cruel hate, the need for vengeance and the cries of pain, the fear of dying and the urge to kill, the brotherless illusion and the self that seemed alone in all the universe. This terrible mistake about yourself the miracle corrects as gently as a loving mother sings her child to rest." (ACIM: C-2.7:6—8:2)

I am deeply comforted by the imagery of the Loving Divine Mother holding and rocking us, singing a soothing lullaby, assuring us that everything is just fine. This is the miracle.

CHAPTER 15

Variations on the Basic True Forgiveness Steps

A Course in Miracles tells us that each being has an individualized curriculum within the universal curriculum that teaches our Perfect Oneness. This means that the Holy Spirit meets us exactly where we believe we are within our perceived narratives. Consequently, there are as many potential methods of True Forgiveness as there are beings appearing in the space-time bubble.

> "The curriculum is highly individualized, and all aspects are under the Holy Spirit's particular care and guidance. Ask and He will answer. The responsibility is His, and He alone is fit to assume it. To do so is His function. To refer the questions to Him is yours. Would you want to be responsible for decisions about which you understand so little? Be glad you have a Teacher Who cannot make a mistake. His answers are always right. Would you say that of yours?" (ACIM: M-29.2:6-14)

Notice that delightful sense of humor? This is a reminder that we forgot to laugh at the tiny, mad idea of separation. We took the OOPS so very seriously, which is what triggered the cascading misperceptions of separation—now the more

Light-hearted we can be on our journey home, the better. Returning to Oneness is a joyful experience, so let's have some fun exploring the various tools in the True Forgiveness toolbelt.

Since the Holy Spirit always meets us where we believe we are in our mental labyrinth, wrapped-up in our imagined fortresses of defense, we can be certain that Spirit always knows the best course of action for our specific situation. If we believe we are suffering, Spirit is with us. If we are doing a joyful happy-dance, Spirit is with us. Every moment of every day and night, Spirit is with us, encouraging us to learn of our Perfect Oneness—Just Ask Spirit, Pause & Listen.

"You can never be alone because the Source of all life

goes with you wherever you go." (ACIM: W-41.4:3) Because Spirit always meets us where we are in our perceived circumstances, there are certain True Forgiveness applications that might feel more resonant to some than to others. Though the Basic True Forgiveness Steps will be effective in any situation, there are times where we may feel guided to modify those steps. As we get more practice, we may not even need to consciously follow each step, they may occur naturally when our mind consistently maintains a state of miracle-readiness. While developing a practice that feels resonant, however, it might be helpful to work with some of the following suggestions:

Nothing real can be threatened — One of the most basic True Forgiveness methods can be simply meditating on the last 3 lines from the Introduction for the Text:

"Nothing real can be threatened. Nothing unreal exists. Herein lies the peace of God."
This might be helpful if something comes up that feels threatening or worrisome.

God Is — Reflecting on the statement found in DU: "God Is and nothing else Is." There are two aspects that are important in this statement. God Is AND there is nothing else that can possibly be real. Anything that is not Loving and Perfect, is not of God, and therefore cannot be true.

Breathwork — Focused breathing is a super-power that will enhance the results of any True Forgiveness process. Certified therapists are available who can facilitate breathwork sessions, which might be something to explore. We can always do our own focused breathing meditations, too—breathwork can be used any time, any where, for free.

Breathwork can help heal a part of our mind that has not seen the Light of Truth for far too long. As long as we are partnered with Spirit to guide our process, True Forgiveness can occur nonverbally, without our directed thought. According to our readiness, some unconscious guilt can simply be skimmed away by Spirit, but some layers will need to be looked at to be released. Either way, breathwork can facilitate Spirit's removal of unconscious debris that is blocking the Light of Truth in our mind.

Pausing & Listening + Breathwork — For an added True Forgiveness benefit, incorporating pauses in our daily mental chatter allows Spirit to communicate with us. By taking time in the day to pause for slow, cleansing breaths, we have the power to change the pace of our thoughts to our preference.

Several ACIM Workbook lessons encourage us to pause from our daily routine which enhances our mind training practices. This strengthens our connection with Spirit and helps miracles unfold naturally.

- "We merely close our eyes, and then forget all that we thought we knew and understood. For thus is freedom given us from all we did not know and failed to understand." (ACIM: W-rVI.in.4:3-4)
- "… we give these times of quiet to the Teacher Who instructs in quiet, speaks of peace, and gives our thoughts whatever meaning they may have." (ACIM: W-rVI.in.6:6)

Mantra: "Cancel, Cancel, Erase, and Replace with Grace" — As one of my favorite Forgiveness statements, I use this when something incongruous seems to occur. It helps me shift from ego-based thinking into Spirit-led, right-minded thinking.

Everyone is a Decorator Crab — In one of my True Forgiveness practices, the Holy Spirit's healing message to me was, Everyone is insecure. My response was, "Ah, I see, of course the separated minds are insecure, we think we lost the safety and protection of our True Home." Every single person we encounter, including oneself, is a walking bundle of insecurities. Remembering this makes it so much easier to use True Forgiveness when we notice defensive behaviors.

After getting this insight, Spirit then showed me a vision of decorator crabs on the ocean floor. These crabs attach objects to their shells that help them hide or defend themselves from predators. Some crabs use toxic sea anemones or spiney urchins; others use seaweed as camouflage; some use colorful seashells. Each crab is highly insecure and vulnerable, but they decorate their shells in different ways to hide themselves and their insecurities.

When I notice my own defensive displays reflected in the people around me, I can understand that we are defensive because we are all terribly insecure. What I find important is that we may be fooled about this, because the defenses can appear in many different ways. One person may be aggressively critical, another is super-shy and skittish, another vainly over-accessorizes. We use different defenses, but underneath, we all feel insecure and that is why we display defenses. And, bringing it full circle, it is our own defensiveness we are seeing in them. If we judge a person based on the decorations they've attached to their outer shells, we are not seeing the real person. When we choose to overlook any type of defenses, we look beyond the outer shell, and we find the innocent Child of God reflecting back to us.

Workbook Lesson 121 — The Course advises us to overlook the behaviors of others, because they have forgotten that they are a Light-filled Child of God. In our mind's eye, we can use our Mom Goggles, also known as Christ's Vision, to perceive the Light within our fellow companions. The Light may seem to be well-hidden, but it is most assuredly there because God's Love is all-encompassing!

Workbook Lesson 121 presents an outline for a beautiful True Forgiveness practice. Think of someone you haven't been getting along with. It could be someone in your work-place, family or social circle. It doesn't matter who is selected, just know that the person who comes to mind is the one to work with at this time.

- Doing breathwork, take time to ground and center and connect with Spirit.
- Identify the feelings and beliefs associated with the person.
- Look at them with Spirit and see that these are ego-based reactions and judgments.
- Perhaps you can see a repeating ego-based pattern from your past experiences.
- Notice that they represent the same reactions you experienced during the OOPS.
- Realize that you have been casting your own shadow on this person, declare that you want to think with your right-mind.
- Close your eyes and picture the person, then Ask Spirit to show you one thing about them that reminds you of their Light within. You don't have to search, it will come to you.
- Imagine this memory as a candle flame shining from their heart.
- Feel your own warm candle flame expanding from your heart, like golden sunbeams.
- Imagine the Light getting brighter as their Light and your Light merge together.
- Notice that your Light and the person's Light are the same Light. It is all the same Divine Love shining from each being.

- Our thoughts become Light-hearted as we breathe in the peaceful feeling of joining with this person.

Using a Dry-Erase Vision Board and Cancel, Cancel, Erase and Replace with Grace

- Work through the Basic True Forgiveness Steps.
- **Step 1: Notice the upset**
- **At Step 2: Notice ego-based patterns,** write down all your associated feelings and beliefs on the dry-erase board with a dry-erase marker.

[Note: When journaling with pen and paper there may be a tendency to avoid writing your deepest "secret sins and hidden hates" because you don't want them to be found later. With the dry-erase board, you can write it ALL down because it will be completely erased very soon.]

- **Step 3: Choose Again, Choose Spirit**
- **At Step 4: Ask Spirit, Pause & Listen,** after breathing & centering, gently erase the upsets written on the board while declaring you are giving all these old patterns to Spirit. This symbolizes our willingness to Cancel, Cancel, Erase them & Replace with Grace.

For the second part of Step 4, after Asking Spirit, Pausing & Listening, write any Spirit-inspired messages on the board that arise in your mind. [Note: I might transfer those inspired messages to paper or a Word doc, but first, I write them on the eraser board.] This symbolically represents Spirit's over-writing of my old stuck patterns based on my erroneous beliefs.

Step 5: Spirit Corrects Intervals of Time

- Erase all of the writings on the board, creating a clean slate for moving forward with more Light shining into your mind.

Freeze frame — [Note: This is a wonderful True Forgiveness practice that I learned from the Circle of Atonement study materials.]

- Think of someone who has upset your peace of mind.
- Form a mental image of their behavior at the height of the emotion, and freeze-frame them in the scene.
- Imagine the person as an outlined cardboard cut-out, like those promotional displays at movie theaters.
- Imagine hinges on one side, then see the cut-out figure swinging open like a door on its hinges.
- As the door swings open, Light spills out from behind the cut-out image of the person who has upset your peace of mind.
- Let the Light expand and fill the freeze-framed scene.
- Let your own Light shine out from behind your own cut-out image.
- Envision your Light merging with theirs in peace and bask in the Light of Truth together.

This exercise allows you to overlook appearances to see the real Son of God behind the facade.

Freeze Film — A variation of this exercise is to imagine a film playing on an old-fashioned projector. You may recall how celluloid film runs from one reel to another reel, causing the film to move past the bright projection lens. As the film moves past the lens, this generates the illusion of movement on the screen, hence the term 'movie.' Sometimes the reel-to-reel spooling mechanism gets stuck, and then the intense heat of the projection light bulb makes the celluloid film melt and burn-up.

I use this imagery as a True Forgiveness method by imagining a movie of the memory or current event being projected onto a big movie screen. My story could depict trauma or regret, injustice or heartache, plus guilt and fear woven into the scene. When I have viewed the film sequence, I acknowledge that I have generated these images from my wrong-mind and projected them onto the screen.

Now that I recognize this, I am ready to switch to my right-mind. With Spirit's help, at the critical moment of the scene playing out, I say "freeze-frame." The film stops, the action freezes like a snapshot on the screen, and then, the intense Light melts the scene that is stopped on the projection lens. It simply burns up and disappears. My great big emotional story turns out to be so flimsy and frail, it melts away in the Light. With the disintegration of the painful images, I feel released from my made-up story.

The Decision for God — This method is derived from the end of chapter 5, Section VII of *A Course in Miracles*. I have found this technique to be one the most effective True Forgiveness processes available. It is very simple, yet earth-shatteringly powerful.

Every day, most of us automatically shut down our feelings and beliefs about difficult situations. Maybe we suppress our reactions because we want to be a 'good person,' so we deny our ugly feelings and unkind judgments. Sometimes we *think* those things but certainly would never say them, yet unspoken grievances are just as damaging—<u>our thought patterns generate our experience in this world</u>. Or, if we do express them, it might happen in a hurtful way, usually because we've been suppressing them for so long, they'll all flood out at once.

We might be tempted to think: *I don't want to give this problem to God, I should be able to fix it myself. I'm ashamed of my behavior. It's unspiritual to feel this way, I can't let God see this ugliness.* But this is exactly what we give to God in order to look at and release our 'secret sins and hidden hates.'

Rather than doing a 'spiritual bypass' by avoiding the emotions, bring it all to God—every bit of seething anger, despondent grief, the deep-seated need for revenge, dark secrets, ugly impulses, all of our wrong-minded judgments. They are all reactions from the OOPS and when we experience them in our sphere of awareness, we can be assured that we are ready to look at them with the Holy Spirit. With all our thoughts that are not joyous, we cast these cares upon the Holy Spirit as they come up in our awareness.

> "You need be neither careful nor careless; you need
> merely cast your cares upon Him because He careth
> for you." (ACIM: T-5.VII.1:4)

We are best served by genuinely looking at our feelings and beliefs when we have a grievance. Keep in mind that we do not try to forgive on our own, we cast our cares upon the Holy Spirit, Ask Spirit, Pause & Listen for healing messages that help us see the situation differently. The more we practice this, the freer and more Light-hearted we become.

"Let us be glad that we can walk the world, and find so many chances to perceive another situation where God's gift can once again be recognized as ours! And thus will all the vestiges of hell, the secret sins and hidden hates be gone. And all the loveliness which they concealed appear like lawns of Heaven to our sight, to lift us high above the thorny roads we travelled on before the Christ appeared." (ACIM: T-31.VIII.9:1-3)

Recall that in the OOPS, when a part of our mind split from Oneness into twoness, we had to decide whether to listen to the ego or the Holy Spirit. In our confusion, we decided wrongly. Since the beginning of space-time, we have believed that because we made that wrong decision, we are bound to it and must live with it forever. Guess what? Good news! Nope! We can decide AGAIN!

"Whenever you are not wholly joyous, it is because you have reacted with a lack of love to one of God's creations. Perceiving this as 'sin' you become defensive because you expect attack. The decision to react in this way is yours, and can therefore be undone. It cannot be undone by repentance in the usual sense, because this implies guilt. If you allow yourself to feel guilty, you will reinforce the error rather than allow it to be undone for you." (ACIM: T-5.VII.5:1-5)

Rather than continuing to feel guilty for deciding wrongly during the OOPS, we simply decide again. This time, we know the Holy Spirit's way is the best way and our decision is certain. As is beautifully outlined at the end of Chapter 5:

"Decision cannot be difficult... Therefore, the first step in the undoing is to recognize that you actively decided wrongly, but can as actively decide otherwise. Be very firm with yourself in this, and keep yourself fully aware that the undoing process, which does not come from you, is nevertheless within you because God placed it there. Your part is merely to return your thinking to the point at which the error was made, and give it over to the Atonement in peace. Say this to yourself as sincerely as you can, remembering that the Holy Spirit will respond fully to your slightest invitation:

I must have decided wrongly, because I am not at peace.

I made the decision myself, but I can also decide otherwise.

I want to decide otherwise, because I want to be at peace.

I do not feel guilty, because the Holy Spirit will undo all the consequences of my wrong decision if I will let Him.

I choose to let Him, by allowing Him to decide for God for me." (ACIM: T-5.VII.6:1-11)

These and many more Miracle Methods that employ True Forgiveness techniques are available to anyone, anywhere, any time. With Spirit's guidance, they can easily be modified to the occasion or need. The Course also tells us it is not necessary to believe that these techniques work for them to be effective. All that is needed is the willingness to try them. It may feel silly or weird at first, but what can it hurt to just explore them? You might even be stunned into speechlessness from the synchronistic results!

CHAPTER 16

Finding Forgiveness Within

THIS chapter presents three examples from my life where I utilized True Forgiveness, which helped me release guilt and fear within my unconscious mind. More and more I am learning that the only reason we seem to see events in the outer world is to get our attention to look at our own unconscious feelings and beliefs.

When something upsets our peace of mind, we take note of our feelings and beliefs associated with the current situation, then, translate those into how we must have reacted during the OOPS. The sooner we recognize that the outer details represent the unconscious condition in need of healing, the faster we advance along our learning path. The challenge is to accept that the person or event that we want to judge as 'bad' is playing a role that causes our unconscious guilt to surface in our awareness.

When blocking the Light of Truth in our mind, we cast a shadow of darkness onto our brother. Once the trigger gets our attention, our own guilt and fear becomes our focus, not the judgment of the person's behavior. It has nothing to do with them anymore. They gave us the cue (that we are ready to look at our own pattern) and the clue (a symbolic snapshot of what our pattern is), and their job is now complete.

Just to be clear, I do not claim to have perfected this technique in my own life, but I am learning more every single day. Each time I practice this, I feel freer and more Lighthearted. I know in my heart of hearts—my right-mind—I am releasing my unconscious blocks to my awareness of God's Perfect, all-encompassing Love.

These Forgiveness stories are intended to encourage people to follow their guidance, partnering with Spirit, Asking, Pausing & Listening. The examples show the progression of the True Forgiveness Steps as well as potential intuitive variations. As I share my own experiences, certain aspects may feel familiar to you—perhaps different details, but there may be a common pattern you recognize. True Forgiveness opportunities arise naturally when we are ready to be healed, so whatever comes up for you while reading this chapter may be an invitation to see your own situation differently, always with Spirit's help.

Sculpture

When this Forgiveness opportunity occurred in 2009, I had been reading *The Disappearance of the Universe* and the Course for about a year. My daughter Miranda, (a.k.a. Mo), was sixteen, my son Brett was eleven, and my youngest son Tiger was ten.

When Mo was in her high school art class, she made a number of beautiful sculptures. One day, she finally brought one of her favorite pieces home—a clay vase with her favorite Marvel Comic symbols sculpted into the graceful curves of the vase. The crowning focal point was a large lid, in the shape of Thor's helmet, that sat on the very top of the vase.

As she placed it on our dining room table, Mo, Brett, Tiger and I were admiring it. As we were taking in all of the intricate details, our youngest son Tiger reached up to touch Thor's helmet. Suddenly, the helmet fell off its perch, tumbled onto the table, and crashed to the floor, shattering into several pieces.

I was shocked and devastated for Miranda. Her masterpiece was in the house for ten minutes and then it was broken into pieces! I was out of my mind with 'upset.' I yelled, "Tiger! Look what you did! You broke it! How could you? Don't mess with other people's things!" My ego-based instincts as a Mother Bear are quite powerful. In my split-second reaction, Mother Bear was lashing out for my daughter's sake. I didn't stop to think that my reaction was harming another of my bear cubs.

The next morning, my husband and I helped Mo glue the pieces back together. I felt guilty and even though I apologized to Tiger, I believed that an apology would not undo the wound that I had caused. He was a ten-year-old kid who was just being a kid. We all want to reach out and touch artwork when we're admiring it. And if the lid was that precarious, it was only a matter of time before it happened. The ego had many justifications for lamenting my outburst against Tiger. Just like Thor's helmet had broken into pieces, I feared I had shattered something in him.

I had been studying the Course for a year, so I recognized that this was an important forgiveness opportunity. At the time, I knew a few things about practicing True Forgiveness, but I was combining the world's version with the Course's very different approach. I put a lot of effort into forgiving my-self, but that simply perpetuated my guilt.

Life went on and the awareness of this guilt slipped into the cellar of my unconscious mind. Maybe it seemed to go away, but any trigger of the event brought it up again, feeling as painful as when it happened. I believed that I had damaged my son's psyche and it was not possible to undo the harm I had caused. Ironically, Tiger barely remembers the incident, though his unconscious surely registered it. We've talked about it over the years, and he has assured me that it is okay. That helped some, but there was still an uncontrollable urge to wade into the quagmire and wallow in the guilt. Have you ever noticed that self-forgiveness feels like the hardest of all forgiveness opportunities?

Keep in mind that all True Forgiveness is actually self-Forgiveness. Any incident draws attention to aspects of our own guilt and fear reactions in the OOPS. We then have an opportunity to forgive our self-imposed guilt and fear, free-ing ourselves from the prison of our separated mind—this is self-Forgiveness each step of the way.

We can tell by the way we feel when the memory is re-played if True Forgiveness has been achieved. When we go over the incident again, if we feel neutral about it, that is a sign that we have let the Holy Spirit heal the unconscious mind of this guilt and false beliefs. If we still feel icky about it, there is more to look at.

The turning point of my guilty self-flagellation occurred about a decade later, as I read the end of ACIM's Chapter 5, The Decision for God. I was stunned when I read the last paragraph:

"I must have decided wrongly, because I am not at peace.

I made the decision myself, but I can also decide otherwise.

I want to decide otherwise, because I want to be at peace.

I do not feel guilty, because the Holy Spirit will undo all the consequences of my wrong decision if I will let Him.

I choose to let Him, by allowing Him to decide for God for me." (ACIM: T-5.VII.6:1-11)

When I got to "I do not feel guilty, because the Holy Spirit will undo all of the consequences of my wrong decision if I will let Him." I gasped. "Wait a minute," then it felt like time stopped and everything literally 'waited a minute' as my mind expanded into this new epiphany. "Do you mean to tell me all the harm can be undone? All the consequences will be entirely undone?" Yes.

Well, that is interesting. All the consequences will be undone—if I will let Him. I definitely was not letting Spirit undo any of the consequences of my wrong decision. When I finally Asked Spirit, Paused & Listened, True Forgiveness simply happened. Here was my thought process:

I must have decided wrongly, because I am not at peace. No, I am definitely not at peace about the harm I believe I caused Tiger with my over-reaction.

I made the decision myself, but I can also decide otherwise. Yeah, I decided to believe the ego's accusations of guilt for verbally attacking Tiger and wounding his psyche. Isn't there a better way than to keep abusing myself with this false memory from the past? Yes there is, I can decide otherwise.

I want to decide otherwise, because I want to be at peace. When the sculpture shattered, I reacted with the ego, blaming and verbally attacking my son, which was a mistake. The ego had baited me, then it turned the tables and blamed me for reacting with the ego. Oh, the irony. This is exactly how the ego tricked us in the OOPS. The ego enticed us to react, and when we did, the ego blamed us for reacting and causing what it told us was irreparable harm. The ego clearly does not have my best interest in mind, but I trust the Holy Spirit to show me the Truth. I know Spirit has a more peaceful way than this. I now want the Peace of God instead of endless self-torment.

I do not feel guilty, because the Holy Spirit will undo all the consequences of my wrong decision if I will let Him. There is no reason to wallow in this quagmire of guilt. The Holy Spirit will undo all the consequences of my wrong decisions. The ego played the long game on me, and I now realize it does not serve me to tolerate that manipulation.

I also recognize that this memory is only a dream sequence depicting my shattering reaction to the Old Original Perceived Separation. In the OOPS, the ego enticed me to separate from God, and then told me I was eternally damned for doing it! Oh, the cosmic irony.

I see it differently now, and you know what—I am so done with that lie. I dreamed I did something harmful, but all that incident did was show me my unconscious guilt in need of healing. It was an opportunity to heal the unhealed mind. And now, I am truly ready for my mind to be healed of this insidious guilt that I chose to cherish for so many years.

I choose to let Him, by allowing Him to decide for God for me. I give Spirit a free access pass to undo ALL the related consequences of that unfortunate series of wrong decisions then, and in the OOPS.

"It must be understood…that whenever you offer a miracle to another, you are shortening the suffering of both of you. This corrects retroactively as well as progressively." (ACIM: T-2.V.10:7-8)

[Note: After writing this, an intuition came that I would get a sign of confirmation that this is so. I said, "Yes, sounds good to me." Just a couple minutes later, when I got up to get a drink, I took two steps and noticed something that made me stop. I was right in front of my bookshelf that holds multiple photos and mementos of our family. Directly at my eye level, next to Tiger's picture, I noticed a plaque that Tiger gave me years ago. It reads, "I Love that you're my Mom."

Thank you, Thank you, Thank you, Spirit... Thank you for this miracle. I'm gonna' go cry this out now—it'll be a good cry, a release, a healing of my heart.]

Paint ball

This True Forgiveness opportunity played out when our middle son Brett was thirteen. We were staying with friends in a nearby town and a friend of theirs had a paintball park on a large, wooded property. We had nearly zero experience playing paintball, but Brett was getting interested in it and he wanted to learn more about it.

Our family of five arrived in our street clothes, and we picked up the equipment and supplies. I had pictured that we would go to a wooded area and our group of friends and family would basically play hide-and-seek with the colorful paintballs.

We rode out in a screened-in trailer and found ourselves in a group with some young Boy Scouts and their leaders, plus about eight other people who were outfitted with camo and equipment. The facilitator explained the rules and then they started the timer for the first game. We figured out very quickly that some of the players were not playing hide-and-seek, but were picking off the 'fresh meat' with precision. They took down the young ones and then worked their way up from there. I was a deer in the headlights, very much out of my element, and wishing it could have been just our families playing.

After a couple of 15-minute rounds, we reset and started the next one. Then there was a commotion in one of the bunkers. My husband and I saw our son Brett coming out of the bunker, then ducking into the screened-in trailer. We found him sitting in the corner, red-faced, struggling not to let tears well-up in his eyes. One of the players, a boy who was about thirteen, had cornered Brett in the stand. Brett had done what you're supposed to do, which is to call "Out." If a player calls "Out" then you can't shoot him. Brett did this, but the kid proceeded to shoot him multiple times at close range and one paintball hit him in the face. Brett was wearing a mask, but the paintball found its way to his cheek, which was dark-red and tear-streaked by now. While we were in the trailer, the kid walked by and boasted to his proud father, "Yeah, I lit him up!"

At this point, Mother Bear was 'loaded for bear,' and about to take down some teen-meat—with precision. Did she do this? No. Why? Because Mother Bear was a student of *A Course in Miracles*.

I knew my ego was spiraling to the extreme and I didn't want to be the 'crazy mom' who fights her son's battles. It was a huge lesson on staying in my lane, and it was not an easy one. I was keenly aware that I would cause more harm and embarrass Brett even more if I unleashed. I remember praying hard to not let one word come out of my mouth, because I could tell this was an ego set-up. As tempted as I was to attack them, I knew that was not the right-minded course of action, so I suppressed everything that I wanted to say to them.

It took me a couple of weeks to process what happened, there were so many aspects of the incident that deeply disturbed my peace of mind. I worked to forgive what I could. Absorbing my rage prevented more damaging fallout, but suppressed rage does not go away, it just festers there in the unconscious.

I think my forgiveness efforts did reduce the intensity of the grievances that arose from this incident. However, I was not following the True Forgiveness steps outlined in the previous chapter, because they didn't appear that way in the ACIM descriptions of the Forgiveness process that I had studied. This is why there are a few more steps in my listing because I find it helpful to process in that way. Consequently, I still didn't understand what miracles were for and how to use them. If we don't have a solid grasp of what, and why, and how, it's much less likely that True Forgiveness will be fully realized.

I had forgotten about the paintball incident for over a decade, but the triggers were alive and well in my unconscious mind. It came up into my awareness while I listened to a Voice Liberation session with Course teacher Neda Boin. When the memory came up, I knew it was time to Truly Forgive it. Now that I understand the process so much better, the results this time were powerfully effective:

1. **Notice the Upset** — The memory came up when I was on a long walk and I was listening to Neda Boin's Voice Liberation session on YouTube.

While listening to Neda guiding the early stage of the session, I noticed a 'vibe' when I saw the green leaves of some holly trees I was walking past. I thought, 'Hmmm, I see something in the leaves (with my mind's eye), what is it?' Then the scene started to emerge of being in the woods at the paintball park.

2. **Notice ego-based patterns** — My feelings and beliefs were multi-layered. My heart was wounded because Brett was hurt, humiliated, and trying not to cry. I wanted to hug him, but I resisted to avoid embarrassing him further. I was deeply indignant because the kid's actions were absolutely intentional. When the kid said he 'lit him up,' vicious rage boiled in my abdomen. He and his father laughed, relishing their 'victory.' Where was the father's integrity? Why didn't he correct his son, knowing what his son did was unethical? I wanted revenge, I wanted to verbally destroy the kid and his father. And then in order avoid embarrassing Brett, I internalized every bit of my rage.

How did this represent the reactions in the OOPS? The ego uses unfair, unethical tactics. We were enticed and then wounded and humiliated by the ego in the separation. We were confused, out-of-our-element, and we did not know what to do. We believed 'The Father' approved the cruelty. The world the ego made for us to hide in is cruel and unjust and we believed we had to live with it. We have to suppress our reactions to the injustice because we believe we have no choice. The game is rigged. Repression of my reactions and strong emotions to the OOPS caused me deep conflict and it had be projected outward, in this case, through projectiles.

The powerful feelings and incorrect beliefs are all the result of listening to the ego's undermining, contradictory nonsense. I believe I have to tolerate it. But do I? I've been reacting with the ego because I have been thinking with my wrong-mind. There has to be a better way.

3. **Choose Again — Choose Spirit —** I would like to look at this with my right-mind. Holy Spirit, please take these false beliefs and help me see this differently.

The Holy Spirit shows me exactly how the ego's game is fixed in a way that no one will ever win. The Holy Spirit gladly takes me by the hand and walks me away from the scenes of my internal war, away from my useless defenses, away from the battle-wounded wasteland of my separated mind. In my imagination, I walk with Spirit into the woods, to a quiet place, far away from the battlefield.

4. **Ask Spirit, Pause & Listen:** In my mind, I am in the woods, everything is still and quiet. The golden sunlight streams in through a canopy of green leaves. I sit at the base of a big, old tree.

Looking up, I search for patches of bright blue sky between the tree branches. I let my mind float upwards to the clouds.

> "The senselessness of conquest is quite apparent from
> the quiet sphere above the battleground."
> (ACIM: T-23.IV.9:5)

I breathe in and out ever so slowly. And I Ask Spirit to take my bitter woundedness to help me see this differently, then I Pause & Listen.

The message that emerges within the silent pause is this: (With certainty, I know this is the message, and I allow it to roll into my heart.) They are my brothers and we are One. In a divisive maneuver, I perceived them to be separate, and I cast my dark shadow of fear onto them. They are Perfect — they just don't know it. They are afraid, so afraid. They conceal their fear with bravado. Help them know there is nothing to fear (powerful shift, and magnetic pull). Help your brothers. Remove the block in your own mind that cast a shadow into their minds. Open your heart and receive the Light you know is there, so they will know it is there. They do not know how to find it. They do not know that fear is the stranger here.

> "I am at home. Fear is the stranger here… Identify
> with fear, and you will be a stranger to yourself."
> (ACIM: W-160.1:1-2)

5. **Spirit Adjusts intervals of Time** — Now that I see this differently, I affirm that I would Love for the Holy Spirit to correct all the related consequences of my error throughout the space-time continuum.

   > "Your brother's errors are not of him, any more than
   > yours are of you. Accept his errors as real, and you
   > Have attacked yourself. If you would find your way

and keep it, see only truth beside you for you walk together. The Holy Spirit in you forgives all things in you and in your brother." (ACIM: T-9.III.7:1-4)

The Spirit of St. Louis

In July 2021, our family and some friends took a road trip to St. Louis. We had a wonderful time together. One of the highlights was the City Museum which is unlike any we've seen before. Anyone with children should go there, and if you don't have children in your home, rent some!

Anyway, one of the must-do things in St. Louis is to go to the Gateway Arch. I'm not sure why I'm drawn to that shiny silver thing, but I like it. When our group went to visit, we were in a bit of a hurry because we were leaving right afterwards for the 7-hour drive home. Our Google map directions put us to the east of the Arch, on a frontage road. I felt anxious because we couldn't see a parking lot close by, so we didn't know where to park.

At the time, cars could parallel park along the frontage road, so that's what we decided to do. Most spaces were taken up, but I saw one and maneuvered to park there. A white van was ahead of me and as it pulled past the spot, I assumed the van was driving past it to another spot. I started to pull in to park, then the white van started backing up to parallel park into the same spot. The driver, a woman in her 60's, rolled her window down and angrily yelled, "Get out of my way!" I shouted back, "I had my signal on!" There was a definite ego-reaction from both of us. My adult children, who were in their own vehicles, saw the exchange.

I remembered to Ask Spirit for help right after my big

emotional spike. I calmed down with focused-breathwork as I drove on, finding another spot further down. Then the kids came up to me and said, "Mom, we saw what happened." I explained that it was just a misunderstanding. She didn't have her signal on so I thought she was driving past the spot, but she was pulling ahead so she could back in. It's okay, we're parked and ready to see the Arch."

Even though I Asked Spirit, then I realized it was a misunderstanding and it was my mistake, there was still an edgy little grievance lurking in my mind when I saw the woman walking up the steps. Isn't it remarkable how our cars and random parking spaces quickly become possessions of the ego identity? The Course tells us that there are no small upsets, they are all equally disturbing to our peace of mind. This came to mind as we ascended the steps to the Gateway Arch, and I knew I had more True Forgiveness Steps to practice in this situation.

First, while my husband was taking group pictures in the grass under the center of the arch, I acknowledged that I obviously had been thinking with the wrong-mind. I Asked Spirit to help me see this differently. And then I was guided to imagine myself high up in the Arch looking down through the windows. From my imaginary window to the world, I viewed the parking lot with tiny cars and people parking, walking around, going up the steps to visit the Arch. I thought, how humorous it must have looked from that high-up window when two little vehicles tried to occupy the same space. From up there, an observer could easily predict the cartoonish conflict that possession of this highly valuable parking spot would bring. I wondered, instead of laying claim to a few square feet of concrete, what if I had simply laughed at myself—laughed at the absurdity of it all?

Later, when we were in the gift shop, I saw the woman sitting alone in the open waiting area nearby. I think one of the kids even said, "Hey, Mom, there she is." Little did they know that I was considering apologizing to her. Fortunately, there was time to work up the courage to do it. I connected with Spirit—my own form of 'liquid courage.' I Asked if this is what I should do in this moment, and the confirmation came into my mind. More a feeling than words, but a definite vibrational sense of, 'It's the right-minded thing to do.' I was entirely unsure how she would react, but my decision was that I would do my part and the rest would not be my concern. I would apologize and if she retaliated, I would simply walk away and not engage her. So, I anchored very firmly with Spirit and made my feet advance forward one step, then another step closer to the woman who was the driver of the white van.

With my heart thudding in my chest, I said a quick "Spirit help," then I approached her from the side. I looked her in the eyes and said, "Hi, I'm the driver who tried to park in your spot. I just wanted to apologize and explain that I didn't realize you were pulling forward so you could back up into the spot. That was my mistake." Immediately, she responded, "Oh my goodness, I am so sorry! I'm driving my friend's van and I don't know how to parallel park. I couldn't see anything when I was backing up. I didn't even know where we were supposed to park. When I yelled at you, my sister said, 'Why do you have to be so mean to people all the time?' I am so sorry, I was a nervous wreck, and I took it out on you!"

Holy Instant on a popsicle stick! Wow! Then we chatted and laughed and had a heartfelt exchange that ended with a hug.

True Forgiveness happens at the level of cause, which is in the mind, so we don't always see the outcome in physical form. Well, this time, the outcome was visible. One of the very best results from this visible outcome is that my kids saw me talking with her, and they were relieved that we were moving forward together happily. Each one of them came up to me at different times and commented that they were glad that it worked out.

> "Our common language lets us speak to all our brothers, and to understand with them forgiveness has been given to us all, and thus we can communicate again." (ACIM: T-30.VII.7:8)

What if I hadn't said anything to her? Think of all the emotions, the guilt and false constructs that would have remained locked in place. In fact, there was something familiar about her energy, and my vibe is that this type of exchange had been a repeating pattern between us from past lives. I think that occurs with more frequency than we realize. It's possible this unhealed wound caused us to orbit each other, and this encounter was another opportunity to heal together. Isn't that interesting? What a huge life lesson!

> "The holiest of all the spots on earth is where an ancient hatred has become a present love." (ACIM, T-26.IX.6:1)

Thank You, Thank You, *Thank You* Spirit of St. Louis!

CHAPTER 17

Forgiveness Ceremony—Atonement

SOMETIMES I feel guided to do the True Forgiveness Steps in the form of a Forgiveness Ceremony. My methods are intuitive and free-form and a ceremony can be used for any number of True Forgiveness projects. When you feel guided to do a ceremony, it can be done anywhere, but I prefer to find a private space where I am not distracted or inhibited by people who are unfamiliar with ceremonies. The process can be deeply personal, and it is good to feel that you can express yourself as needed.

When I feel inspired to do a Forgiveness Ceremony, I pack a little tote bag with several items. I never know what tools I will be guided to use in the spontaneously unfolding ceremony, so I like to have options prepared. I include a water bottle, paper, pencil, bowl, tweezers, two lighters, candles, a mortar and pestle, a metal singing bowl and handle, scissors, a feather, sage, Young Living essential oils, as well as bug repellant, if I'm headed out to the woods. [Note: Bowl and tweezers are needed to safely hold scraps of paper to burn, and the two lighters are in case one lighter runs low on lighter fluid.]

If going to the wooded location that I like to visit, I set up a lawn chair and place the items on the flat surface of a concrete bench. I might play peaceful music on my phone. Next is grounding with my shoes off. I make direct contact with the good earth, as I breathe slowly in and out. I tune-in to the sounds of the birds, the creek, the squirrels, the breeze in the trees. I like to look up at the blue sky and white clouds. I especially love to see the stars if the timing is right. This helps me connect with a Higher perspective, so I can see the forest from above the trees.

As I breathe all of this in, gratitude rises from my heart-space for the ever-present Essence that supports us. As I find a stillness within, I Ask Spirit, Pause & Listen, awaiting any messages. Often the Forgiveness opportunity is ready to come forward. Then I usually follow each progressive True Forgiveness Step, taking notes when guided to.

- Once the notes are written, I Ask Spirit to read over the notes with me. Then I say to Spirit, "Because I have been thinking with my wrong-mind, I made up all of these feelings and beliefs. I see now that they have not served me. I want to give all of this to you, Spirit. I Ask you to help me see this with my right-mind, that I may see this differently."

- I Pause & Listen to any messages, images, feelings or sensations that occur during the silence. Usually, it is a completely unexpected insight that comes through me. Sometimes it seems like there isn't much coming through, so I just bask in the peacefulness. Sometimes it is just the littlest glimpse of an image or thought. Seemingly insignificant, but when I receive that little inkling, then it expands. Sometimes it is something that I think isn't relevant, but I acknowledge it, keeping faith that it very likely will make more sense later.

- If guided to, I take the notes with my ego-based feelings and beliefs and physically undo them by gently tearing them up or burning them, or both. It's important to do this from a peaceful place. If there is animosity toward my wrong beliefs, that could reinforce them. I watch the words dissolve as the paper burns. I observe the smoke gently wafting up in circles, up, up and away.

- Sometimes I take the ashes of the papers, put them in the mortar dish, and use the pestle to turn them into a powder. Then I will empty the bowl into the creek, saying goodbye to those false ideas, and watching the ashes float down and wash away in the gentle current.

- I might be prompted to read a poem or the daily lesson, or do some tai chi, stretching, breathwork, Voice Liberation, feel the sunshine warming my skin, silent sitting, guided imagery, or repeat a mantra, such as: "I am an innocent Child of God."

- When it is time to conclude the ceremony, I Ask Spirit, Pause & Listen. Whenever I do, I receive a short phrase. Whatever it is, I repeat it slowly. For I know it is meant for this moment, and for moving forward. It can be called on whenever I feel prompted.

These are the primary features of my Forgiveness ceremonies. Of course the variations are endless, as long as they do no harm to myself or anyone else, and they follow some form of the True Forgiveness Steps.

The following is a description of the True Forgiveness ceremony that I performed to heal my unconscious anger about the traditional religious meaning of the Atonement. In chapter 3, Language Baggage, I described how ACIM expands the meaning of traditional religious terms. As I was writing that chapter, everything was going along nicely, until I began discussing the traditional connotations of the word Atonement. Here is what I wrote:

"One of the most important examples of a potentially charged biblical term is 'the Atonement.' ACIM uses this concept in a completely different way than how we typically think of it. According to traditional interpretations of the Bible, it is believed that all of humanity has sinned against God. In order to avoid eternal damnation, this wrathful God demanded retribution for our transgressions. Consequently, Jesus had to be crucified so the innocent blood of the sacrificial lamb 'atoned' for all our sins."

As I started to describe these old biblical connotations, very unexpectedly, a wave of hateful indignation made its way up from my unconscious mind. I felt the dizzying surge of anger rise up like a tsunami from my abdomen up to my throat and then my head. I was thinking how religious powers-that-be distorted the Loving messages of the Bible and used its hypocritical aspects to threaten and manipulate people through guilt.

First they claim that an angry God demanded to have an innocent man sacrificed, to 'atone' for our sins. Then they invoke the fear of God in us, telling us we are unworthy sinners who will burn in hell if we don't atone for our sins. Where is God's all-encompassing Love in this scenario? I felt an ancient anger against this manipulative mentality that has justified murder and cruelty in the name of God for centuries. My perception of the complete wrongness of those misinterpretations runs very deep in my psyche. Yet I know that it is my own guilt and fear that I've projected away from me.

I also felt that this intense reaction is probably connected with past life experiences. I got the sense that at the level of form there was a long-repeated pattern of suffering at the hands of religious powers-that-be, and it had not ended well.

When I felt my emotions surging, I immediately Asked Spirit for guidance. The message was to take a few minutes to explore the feelings and beliefs then give them over to Spirit. I felt a shift and the feelings ebbed in that moment, but I knew this was deep and a True Forgiveness ceremony would help me process this further.

When it was time for the ceremony, I gathered my supplies, just as described at the first of this section, except I couldn't find my mortar bowl. I searched several areas, but it was not to be found. I surrendered this little detail and then Asked Spirit to guide the flow of what was to happen, affirming that everything I did would be done from inner-prompts from my right-mind. Everything that I experienced was unexpected, unplanned, and I didn't know where it was going, I just followed, and followed some more. I began with grounding, centering and slow breathing. I tuned-in to the natural sounds of the wooded area.

Then I lit a candle to indicate the beginning of the True Forgiveness ceremony. Opening an essential oil blend called Gathering, I let a couple of drops fall into the melted candle wax, letting the flame send the aroma into the air as a Calling-in of Love for the ceremony. As I began the True Forgiveness Steps, I reviewed the experience I had while writing several months before:

1. **Notice the upset** — When I was writing about the biblical connotation of the Atonement, anger rose up from my
   subconscious mind. I knew this was a good opportunity
   to use True Forgiveness Steps.

2. **Notice my feelings and beliefs, ego reactions and translate into the OOPS reaction** — "I am bitterly resentful of
   the church and their guilt-inducing tactics, making people believe they are hopeless sinners in need of Atonement, or suffer eternal damnation at the Hand of a wrathful God who demanded the innocent blood of the lamb.
   The misinterpretations and manipulation of scriptures.
   I really, really hate them, judging and murdering in the
   name of God, justifying it in the name of vengeance. The
   corruption and abuse of power. The abuse of children.
   The history—the Crusades, witch burning, execution of
   scientists who reported their findings. Etc, etc, etc."

When my intense reaction came up months before, these hidden hates reflected in my body with physical reactions such
as piercing pain in my abdomen; tension surging upward
from my solar plexus, anger clamping in my throat, and diz-
ziness and heat rose up to my face. I made notes of these, too,
although I only had burning abdominal pain at the time of
the ceremony, which disappeared afterwards.

- **How does this represent my own guilt and fear?** I have
  persecuted myself since the OOPS and I feel so wounded
  by this. I believed the ego's lies and allowed myself to be
  controlled and manipulated, because I have believed every story listed above has actually happened. I did this to

myself. I projected blame onto everyone and everything to get rid of it in myself.

- **Relate feelings and beliefs to the OOPS** — As I reviewed the unethical behaviors of certain religious institutions, I saw a pattern: Lies, corruption, judgment, trauma, ostracization, manipulation, guilt and fear-mongering threats. All of those patterns describe the ego's tactics during the OOPS! That's it! The old interpretation of the Atonement—the innocent blood of the lamb being sacrificed to keep an angry God from punishing sinners—is such an ego distortion of the Truth that the Bible does contain. Then I heard a message in response to that insight: All the Atonement really means is, "Cancel, Cancel, Erase false beliefs and Replace with Grace." Well that makes it much easier to understand!

3. **Choose Again — Choose Spirit** — Because there was not ever any separation, my feelings and beliefs are not correct, and thinking with my wrong-mind has not served me. My mind made a hellish nightmare that I believed was real. I give all these false feelings and beliefs to you Spirit. I want to switch to thinking with my right-mind, that I may view the Truth with Christ's Vision. I choose You, Spirit.

4. **Ask Spirit, Pause & Listen, Paradigm Shift** — I Asked Spirit to help me see this with my right-mind, and I Paused & Listened. Then a message gradually came to me: "Take… down… the… wall."

It took me a few seconds to connect with the meaning. Then the image came to me that I had walled-off my heart with all of my indignant judgments about the ego's religious guilt and fear-mongering that has seemed to go on for eons. In my mind's eye, I saw that each stone I used to make the wall had a word on it. I picked up a lined index card and drew vertical lines to replicate the appearance of a wall of stones. On each 'stone' I wrote a word, such as Atonement, sinner, guilt, wrath, execution, blasphemy, etc.

I wrote about fifty words on the card that represented the ego's religious distortion of God's eternal all-encompassing Love for us. I affirmed that these were false beliefs that did not serve me; and that my judgment regarding the corruption of certain religious institutions was also false and not serving me. I stated, "These feelings and false beliefs do not serve." I then held up the index card of religiously-charged words, lit the corner of it, setting it in a bowl while it burned up. I affirmed that I did not want that wall around my heart. I watched as each word on each stone on the card was dispelled into ashes. The last word to burn, on the upper left corner of the card, was 'ego.' Then the whole card became nothing but frail ashes.

I felt it would be helpful for me to imagine removing the stones from my wall, so I envisioned taking down the wall of hurts and hates around my heart that I had built up, one stone at a time. When I imagined taking a heavy stone off the wall, I read the religious word written on each one, then the stone became lighter and lighter as I handed it up to Yeshua to take it away for me. Yeshua, my brother, whose Love for me is unconditional. Eventually, every stone was taken down from the wall of religious hurt and hate that stood as my defense against God's Love since time began. Every single stone.

5. **The Holy Spirit Adjusts Time** —The Holy Spirit undoes all the consequences of my error throughout the space-time continuum.

After affirming the Holy Spirit's correction of all my related errors throughout time, I peacefully burned all of the note-cards and poured the ashes into a metal singing bowl, rather than the mortar, because I couldn't find the mortar bowl that morning. I used the pestle to gently break them down into powder. Then I used a wooden handle to tap the outside edge of the curved metal, causing it to ring with a deep resonance. Then I ran the handle around the edge to carry over the vibrations into a long hum. As I rotated it around and around, I envisioned that the ashes were becoming purified. Any lingering vibration of the ego's influence was dispelled as the frequency was raised. Then I was drawn to tap the metal edge again several times. I thought, *What does that sound remind me of?* In another epiphany, I heard church bells ringing in my mind. I tapped several more times, rejoicing and embracing the new healing resonance of the ringing church bells. What the ego distorted in churches throughout history, which is a false illusion anyway, I do not have to let come between me and my God. Ring it out! Sing it out! Bring it out! Celebrate the opening of Communication with God because Yeshua and I took the wall down!

I realized why I couldn't find the mortar that morning, the ashes needed to go into the metal singing bowl for those resonant insights to come to me. Then I stood and peacefully poured the ashes over the drop-off where the creek meanders below. The tiny particles gracefully floated down into the gently-flowing water. I watched as the powdered ash was carried away on the current, around the corner and gone. Peacefully gone.

To conclude the ceremony, I reflected on all of the good that churches have served in communities. They have grown Love; they've shared messages of hope; brought music to the spheres; been a gathering space for meals, celebrations and memorials; provided shelter and safety in times of need; helped heal people at all levels, physically, mentally, emotionally, spiritually. Yes, religions and their churches have grown Love.

I Asked Spirit what I should close with. I pulled a blank card and wrote 'God Is.' I thought perhaps that is all to write. But then so many ideas came to me, I wrote each one down: Light, Peace, Joy, Extension, Creator, Source, Amorphous, Ecstasy, Joined, Eternal, Changeless, Limitless, Perfect, Smiling, Tranquil, Absolute Still-Point, Holy, All-Encompassing Love… God Is.

"When you have looked on what seemed terrifying, and seen it change to sights of loveliness and peace; when you have looked on scenes of violence and death, and watched them change to quiet views of gardens under open skies, with clear, life-giving water running happily beside them in dancing brooks that never waste away; who need persuade you to accept the gift of vision?" (ACIM: T-20.VIII.11:1)

CHAPTER 18

Homeward Bound

Our mind has incredible creative powers, and our thoughts direct how those creative powers are expressed. Dwelling in Oneness, our natural state is to generate endlessly beautiful creations extending our Oneness. In the split mind, our creative powers have been misappropriated by the ego to generate a dream of false experiences of separation. The experience in our space-time bubble feels very real, but in terms of the ultimate reality, is it not true. If we want to change our experience from one of separation to one of joining, it is critically important to fully understand that our own thoughts are continually generating our experience.

Think of a machine that continuously sends a stream of bubbles into the air. It can be mesmerizing to watch the bubbles floating everywhere, eventually popping as they land on the ground. If you think about it, our mind generates thoughts like a bubble machine continuously pumping out thoughts. We can envision this by imagining a bubble machine on the top of our head — see the ongoing stream of thought bubbles emerging and floating around?

There's another detail to add to the vision. If our thoughts are coming from our wrong-mind, what kind of bubbles are being generated? They might be a smoggy grey, and when they pop, a toxic acid disintegrates whatever they land on.

Now imagine the clarity of thought bubbles coming from our right-mind. They're clean and clear and contain Light that expands, shining outward wherever they land. These Light bubbles create ripple effects which resonate throughout the multiverse and beyond.

There's one more feature of our bubble machine to consider. Whether we realize it or not, *we walk into* the thought bubbles that we generate, either from our wrong-mind or our right-mind. We experience the effects that our thought bubbles produce, and those effects are either miserable or enjoyable. Our free will ensures that we can always choose which part of our split mind we think with. We can pump out ugly bubbles, but we'll walk right into their toxic effects. Or we can choose to produce purified thought bubbles from our right-mind, walking into the Light of Truth as we do so. The power of decision is ours, and these are the two choices that are available to us.

> "The power of decision is your one remaining free-
> dom as a prisoner of this world. You can decide to
> see it right." (ACIM: T-12.VII.9:1-2)

When we look at our toxic wrong-minded thought bubbles with Spirit, we are able to see them differently and we realize what we believed to be 'bad' is simply false. Then Spirit dispels the false and the Truth transforms into a clear Light bubble that shines on everyone equally. That is the paradigm shift of the miracle.

Since we have accrued many layers of fearful defenses, it is usually a gradual process to undo them as we allow each layer to be dispelled. As long as we are harboring our guilt and fear within our unconscious mind, conflict will be projected onto others in the external world. Whenever we experience challenging times, it is helpful to remember these are prime opportunities to apply the True Forgiveness steps. For most people, when we are caught-up in judging someone, it takes practice to remember to Ask Spirit, Pause & Listen. When we do remember, we can then apply the steps of True Forgiveness. Knowing the upset is an opportunity to look at our own guilt and fear with Spirit, often helps problems resolve much more quickly.

Though the process of removing our barriers to God's Love can take years, when we experience miracles, our lives often transform so powerfully we know we are on the right track. When we allow Spirit to gently remove our barriers to God's Love, the Light of Truth shines from within us in all directions, dispelling our belief in the guilt of others. We accomplish this by following the Holy Spirit's gentle step-by-step guidance, which propels us on our pathway back to our True Home. Together Is Home.

> "You and your brother are coming home together, after a long and meaningless journey that you undertook apart, and that led nowhere. You have found your brother, and you will light each other's way. And from this light will the Great Rays extend back into darkness and forward unto God, to shine away the past and so make room for His eternal Presence, in which everything is radiant in the light." (ACIM: T-18.III.8:5-7)

APPENDIX

Perspectives on Study Methods
& Recommended Reading List

As a student of the Course since 2008, I have discovered some helpful resources that support my ongoing learning journey. This appendix is a compilation of recommended reading materials, study habits and links to explore as you feel drawn to do so. The information included here is current as of this printing. Check my website *larapollock.com* for updates, as needed in the future.

Gradual Accumulation of ACIM Wisdom Over Time

Course teacher Ken Wapnick explained that while our intellectual mind may not fully understand, our subconscious mind integrates ACIM concepts over time. My advice is to keep an open mind and try not to struggle with what doesn't make sense. Ask Spirit to help the understanding come to you and give it time to coalesce.

Digital Search

When I would like to learn more about a particular ACIM term, I search the digital version of the FIP edition or the COA's CE app. Pulling up the related ACIM lines can be helpful because it lets the meaning come through from the actual source.

For the FIP, I start with *acim.org*, click on 'Read ACIM', then 'Entire ACIM Web Edition', and then I use the search feature. If I still can't locate the specific phrase that I have in mind, I'll try *acimi.com* and search 'exact phrase.' For COA searches, download the CE app from *acimce.app*. It takes a little time to learn the search parameters for each website, but I find using digital search features very worthwhile.

One feature of the FIP & COA versions is that they automatically cite the chapter, section and lines of the quote when you transfer it into a document. For example, if you want to share an ACIM quote in an email, it is simple to incorporate by highlighting, copying and pasting. The quote will be cited when you paste it. Easy-peasy!

Religious insights from ACIM study

A comment about ACIM in general, and the COA book in particular, is that it helps reconcile some of the dualistic passages of the Bible into more accurate, nondualistic meanings. When I first started reading the Course, I was not a fan of the Bible, churches, Jesus or God. I automatically rejected most biblical passages as dualistic and misleading. After studying the Course, I've learned to appreciate many of the Bible's healing messages because ACIM explains them how they were meant to be understood.

> "I cannot choose for you, but I can help you make your own right choice. 'Many are called but few are chosen' should be, 'All are called but few choose to listen.' Therefore, they do not choose right. The 'chosen

ones' are merely those who choose right sooner."
(ACIM: T-3.IV.7:11-14)
In addition, the purple COA version is annotated with commentary from Robert Perry and several of his notes help reconcile biblical references into nondualistic messages. After years of ACIM study, I'm pleasantly surprised that my attitude of outright disgust with religious references has transformed to genuine appreciation—and that is a miracle!

Daily Course Practices

"If you have made it a habit to ask for help when and where you can, you can be confident that wisdom will be given you when you need it. Prepare for this each morning, remember God when you can throughout the day, ask the Holy Spirit's help when it is feasible to do so, and thank Him for His guidance at night. And your confidence will be well founded indeed." (ACIM: M-29.5:8-10)

The following describes the ACIM-related activities I include in my day. It has taken me years to incorporate these regular practices into my schedule, and each is shared here as a little possibility to try that may enhance your learning journey.

Join with Spirit Upon Awakening — In the morning when I first wake up, I try to remember to connect with Spirit. I say something like, "Spirit, Here I am. I appreciate your guidance throughout the day." If I feel the prompt to go deeper into my surrender of the day, I will do so.

Reading Daily Lesson from the Workbook —The Workbook has 365 lessons to help students learn the messages of the Course. The daily lessons start on January 1st and go through December 31ˢᵗ, and the Workbook instructs that we do only one lesson per day. [Note: When there's a leap year, we just repeat the lesson that corresponds to February 28ᵗʰ on February 29ᵗʰ.] In the morning, after connecting with Spirit, I read the printed words at the same time the lesson is being read on an audio link, I get much more out of it this way. [Note: James Twyman has recorded a lovely musical version of each ACIM Workbook lesson, which can be pulled up on YouTube.] It also can be helpful to say the words aloud, this adds a vibrational component as a ripple effect in the whole learning process.

- Keeping on-track with the lessons—I find it's much easier to keep track of which lesson I'm on when I do the daily calendar lesson. And each year that I return to the lesson, there is so much more depth of understanding. [Note: If you are interested in starting the Workbook, regardless of what time of year it is, it might be best to start at the first lesson and do one each day until December 31ˢᵗ. Then start over with Lesson 1 and follow the calendar lessons from there.]

- FIP Access to the daily calendar lesson—The FIP website, *acim.org*, has the daily lesson link towards the bottom of the 'Entire ACIM Web Edition' page. I use an app on my phone to pull it up. An audio recording of every lesson is also available on the app and website.

- Some study groups will email or text the lesson each day if you sign up for it.

Using My Dry-erase Vision Board for True Forgiveness — When I return from my walk, I sit and write any feelings and beliefs that are coming up for me in that moment. When

I'm done, I affirm with Spirit that we are *erasing* all of my false beliefs, my regrets and resentments, everything that has come up for me in that moment—the slate is now clean, and I am ready to write the healing messages that arise when I Ask Spirit, Pause & Listen. My True Forgiveness insights have grown exponentially since I have added this to my ACIM-filled day.

Listening to Neda Boin's Music — One of my favorite rituals as I prepare breakfast is to listen to one or both of Neda Boin's beautiful CD's, *The Light Has Come* and *Remember You're Dreaming*, also available on YouTube and her website, *nedaboin.com*.

Reading and Listening to Course-Related Material in the Day — I often use an earbud to listen to an ACIM-related link while on a walk or doing tasks. Some of my favorite links are listed below under 'Course-Related Audiovisual Links.'

Pausing for the Daily Lesson During the Day — The instructions within the lessons usually encourage us to pause to reflect on the idea for the day, occasionally stopping what we are doing to meditate on the lesson. Most students don't remember to repeat the lesson's idea for the day every time, and that's okay—it is not something to feel guilty about, we just do the best we can and get better with practice.

Weekly ACIM Study Group Meetings — An ACIM-related activity that I make top priority is meeting regularly with a group of trusted people who are equally committed to learning the healing messages of the Course. Currently I am co-leading a study group through Unity that meets two times a week. I also meet weekly with a small group of trusted friends who study the COA's materials.

Being Miracle-Ready in the Day — The mindset of an ACIM student is different than most of the people we encounter. Our goal is to maintain a set-point of being connected with Spirit, applying True Forgiveness in whatever ways are feasible at the time.

Forgiveness opportunities can crop up in so many different ways, it's good to recognize them as soon as possible when they play out in the day. Whenever I see people, I try to view them through my Mom-Goggles. I look for the Light within them, I shine my Light from within me, and most importantly, I affirm that our Light is exactly the same Light.

I am not always perfect in applying these practices. When I find myself judging people, I try to switch from my wrong-mind to my right-mind. It is a learning process to look past any disharmonious behaviors to find the harmonious True Light within them. As a form of True Forgiveness, I feel this is the most worthwhile activity in the entire world!

Bedtime Reflections — When going to bed, reviewing the daily lesson reinforces the messages before going to sleep. Then I might listen to a Course-related talk that helps me relax and drift off to sleep. If I read a book at bedtime, it is usually either the Course, or a Course-related book. My intention is to surrender even my nighttime hours to the healing of the mind that believes in the separation.

> "The mind is very powerful, and never loses its creative force. It never sleeps. Every instant it is creating." (ACIM: T-2.VI.9:5-7)

Dream journaling — The mind is generating thoughts and communicating every second of the day and night. So even while we sleep, there are opportunities to learn of our return path to our Home in God. The first few chapters of the COA refer to the levels of consciousness. The superconscious and the subconscious levels of our mind are sending Loving and joining messages to our conscious mind and dreams are an excellent learning venue, if we are open to exploring the symbolic meanings of our dreams. Dreams that seem to be bad may actually be distorted healing messages. These healing messages come up from the miracle impulse of our deep subconscious mind, but they must navigate through our superficial unconscious mind that houses our guilt and fear. The polluted debris field of the unconscious can cause the pure miracle impulse to arise in the consciousness in a distorted or disturbing manner. Asking Spirit can help sort those messages out.

Dream journaling has tremendous potential to help us understand our innocence, teach us True Forgiveness and receive messages of encouragement. You can keep a notebook by your bed or use a voice recording app to describe your dreams, transferring the details to a written document when you have time. Though not a student of the Course, author Robert Moss has excellent insights on the use of dreams for our healing journey, I highly recommend his books.

Course-Related Audiovisual Links — One study method that I Love is listening to a podcast or YouTube link while I am walking, doing tasks, or drifting off to sleep. This helps reinforce the foundational messages of the Course. Often just one little detail in the discussion helps a miracle unfold in my mind with an 'a-ha' moment. The following is a listing of digital resources and teachers that I frequently listen to.

- *Foundation for Inner Peace ACIM audio recordings (acim.org)* — The Foundation for Inner Peace has all of the Workbook Lessons recorded, as well as their "Let's Discuss" webinars; their Text audiolinks are on YouTube.
- *Miracle Voices (miraclevoices.org)* — Originally, this podcast was co-hosted by Mathew McCabe and the amazing Judith Skutch Whitson, who was one of the original co-founders of The Foundation for Inner Peace, which first published *A Course in Miracles* in 1976. Judy passed away in 2021 and now her daughter, Tam Morgan, who is the current president of FIP, co-hosts with Matt. I recommend listening to these in order, from the first episode onward, which gives listeners an opportunity to learn about Judy's incredible contributions to the publication and distribution of the Course. I enjoy these podcasts because their emphasis is on stories of True Forgiveness. They interview Course Students from around the world, and each guest shares their Forgiveness experiences and how they are applying the Course teachings in their lives.
- *Circle of Atonement (circleofa.org)* — this is the organization that has published the purple COA book, the CE, which is based on a transcription of Helen's original handwritten notes. Robert Perry is a COA founder and Emily Bennington is currently the executive director of the organization. The COA website contains numerous resources that facilitate the study of *A Course in Miracles*.

ACIM Teachers — Most of these teachers have posts on social media platforms such as YouTube, so you can listen and decide if you resonate with their approach to teaching ACIM.

Ken Wapnick *(facim.org)* — Ken is known as the first teacher of the Course. After Helen and Bill completed the scribing of ACIM, they met Ken who worked with Helen to edit and prepare the manuscript for publication through the Foundation for Inner Peace. Though he passed in 2013, he wrote over thirty books, produced 225+ recordings and taught for over thirty-five years. He emphasized the metaphysics of ACIM which can be difficult to grasp from our viewpoint in the physical world.

Gary Renard and **Cindy Lora-Renard** *(garyrenard.com and cindylora.com)* — As ACIM teaching partners, Gary and Cindy focus on applying the main Course message of practicing True Forgiveness in our daily lives. Gary is the author of *The Disappearance of the Universe*, and he and Cindy have written more books since then. They also hold online and in-person workshops.

David Hoffmeister and Frances Xu *(davidhoffmeister.com)* — These are a couple of my favorite teachers because they are so balanced and supportive of everyone's process. As I listen to their talks on my walks, I appreciate their gentle laughter and peaceful approach while still addressing the need for True Forgiveness to release our unconscious guilt.

They have numerous links on YouTube and if you explore their main website, check out all of their activities, retreats, books, teaching materials and the Movie Watcher's Guide to Enlightenment (MWGE). In the Movie Watcher's audio links, David uses movie plots to explain the teachings of the Course, helping to make ACIM concepts more relatable in our lives, and that is very important. If we don't resonate with the application of the concepts, we delay our healing process. It's fine to delay, there's no judgment, it just isn't fun to experience more self-induced suffering, due to our belief in separation, when it isn't necessary.

Also, David's Levels of Mind diagram and the Instrument for Peace worksheet are particularly helpful and they can be accessed at *levelsofmind.com*. These resources provide a nice system for practicing True Forgiveness.

Neda Boin (*nedaboin.com*) — Another outstanding teacher is Neda Boin from Rotterdam, Holland. I first met her in 2019 at the International ACIM conference in Boston. Little did I know when I bought her CD at the conference how much that ten-dollar purchase would impact my life.

She also offers an amazing and practical method for True Forgiveness called Voice Liberation. This practice helps us heal our unconscious emotional wounds which block our awareness of God's ever-present Love. She has even developed her own Voice Liberation Community with excellent resources for applying True Forgiveness practices. I have attended amazing retreats with Neda leading Voice Liberation and the potential for healing is profound.

Nouk Sanchez and **Coreen Walson** (*nouksanchez.com*) — A teaching team who have a program called the Total Transformation Course that contains seven keys to authentic relating. The learning from their program can be powerful and deeply healing. They also have recorded intuitively unpacked discussions of each of the Workbook lessons which can be accessed on YouTube.

Diederik Wolsak (*diederik.org*) — His book and program for healing the mind is titled *Choose Again — The Six Steps to Freedom*. He also is the founder of the Choose Again Attitudinal

Healing Centres in Vancouver and Costa Rica. His emphasis is on healing interpersonal relationships and recovering from substance abuse. Diederik's teachings embody True Forgiveness processes and can be incredibly life-changing. Interestingly, his philosophy is ACIM-based but he does not directly reference it in his materials. This might be appealing to people who prefer learning ACIM concepts without some of the potentially off-putting language of the Course.

Study Groups — Another option for beginning, returning, and long-time students, is to sign up for an ACIM study group. They can be extremely helpful in learning ACIM concepts. For me, the best approach is to regularly study the Course by myself and also attend a group once or twice a week.

There are many options for finding a study group, but before going over them, I want to share a potential pitfall of study groups. Because study group members come from very different backgrounds, people may have differing ideas about what the Course is saying. Sometimes everyone is on the same page and even if someone does not see it the same way, the group honors where the person is in their learning journey. However, sometimes a student may monopolize the group, imposing their interpretation of the Course onto other students. I have experienced this and, though the experience provides copious True Forgiveness opportunities, I believe there is only so much of that dynamic that should be tolerated. This shouldn't deter you from looking for a study group, it is just something to be aware of.

There are many options for finding supportive study groups. I recommend trying them out and continuing to look until you find a good fit for you. To determine if a study group is right for you, pay attention to how you feel before, during and after the meetings. Connect with Spirit to get a sense of the dynamics. Are you looking forward to attending the meeting? Do you feel it is a safe space to share the memories and emotions that are coming up? Afterwards, do you feel edified? This is not to say that the expectation should be to always have happy experiences in the meetings. But it is important to discern whether the overall effect feels healing and helpful to you.

The Foundation for Inner Peace has a global map with links for active study groups. Many Unity churches around the world sponsor ACIM study groups. The Circle of Atonement also lists groups who emphasize study of the purple COA book.

Some study groups are unstructured and involve talking about random examples of applying ACIM principles. In some groups, participants take turns reading through the Course, maybe a paragraph at a time, then discussing the meaning found there. Some groups, such as Circle of Atonement, are much more structured and use formatted study materials. This could be a good option for new students because the summarized explanations of the sections can be quite helpful. In addition, the COA discussion questions help students apply the learning to examples from their personal experiences.

Each type of group has its advantages and potential disadvantages. I suggest trying a few different groups to see what you prefer. And I would also say, do not obligate yourself to continue with any study group that does not suit your needs. My best advice, as always, is to Ask Spirit, Pause &

Listen to your guidance.

ACIM-related Retreats — I highly recommend participating in a Course-related retreat. It's a great way to connect with students from around the world, and healing retreats provide wonderful opportunities for processing unconscious guilt and fear. The supportive environment may allow the guilt and fear to be expressed from a deeper level. ACIM retreats can be truly life-changing, so if you feel drawn to attend one, Ask Spirit, Pause & Listen!

RECOMMENDED READING LIST

Many of these authors have more books available, as well as social media platforms, which are worth checking out.

COURSE-RELATED BOOKS & AUTHORS

The Disappearance of the Universe — Gary Renard

Your Immortal Reality — Gary Renard

Love Has Forgotten No One — Gary Renard

The Lifetimes When Jesus and Buddha Knew Each Other — Gary Renard

The Business of Forgiveness — Cindy Lora-Renard

A Course in Health and Wellness — Cindy Lora-Renard

Understanding A Course in Miracles — D. Patrick Miller

Never Forget to Laugh — Carol Howe

Absence from Felicity — Ken Wapnick

Non-Course Books & Authors

Though these are not specifically Course-related, the first eleven authors listed helped form my foundation of understanding, preparing the way for the Course to become my life's Calling. I primarily read Course-related materials now, but there might be something on this list that provides a helpful insight for understanding *A Course in Miracles*.

- *There is a River: The Story of Edgar Cayce* — Thomas Sugrue
- *Black Elk Speaks* — John Neihardt
- *The Celestine Prophecy* — James Redfield
- *Holographic Universe* — Michael Talbot
- *Forever You* — T. Lobsong Rampa (+ many more books)
- *Living in the Light* — Shakti Gawain (+ many more books)
- *Science of Mind* — Ernest Holmes
- *Zen Physics* — David Darling
- *Journey of Souls & Destiny of Souls* — Michael Newton
- *Initiation* — Elizabeth Haich
- *The Power of Now* and *A New Earth* — Eckhart Tolle

Proof of Heaven — Dr. Eben Alexander

Wolf's Message — Suzanne Giesemann

Loving What Is — The Revolutionary Process Called "The Work"
    — Byron Katie

The Four Agreements — Miguel Ruiz

Conscious Dreaming — Robert Moss (+ many more books)

ABOUT THE AUTHOR

Lara Pollock was born in San Antonio where she spent the first seven years of her childhood. Then in 1975, her family moved to Wichita, Kansas, where she has lived since then.

Being a sensitive-intuitive, Lara was often overwhelmed by the unkind ways of the world. Gradually she learned to manage her empathic abilities in such a way that she could serve the greater good. Lara feels her greatest good has been raising three amazing kids with her husband Danny.

Additionally, Lara followed a widely varied career pathway, starting as a dental assistant through high school and college as she trained for English education. From there she practiced therapeutic massage, facilitating hands-on healing, and teaching therapeutic massage classes. In 2005, she began training as a practitioner of Traditional Chinese Medicine (TCM), including acupuncture and herbology.

In 2008, Lara's life transformed as she discovered the great wisdom teaching *A Course in Miracles*. Since then, in each of her roles in life, Lara's underlying goal has been to demonstrate the principles of ACIM, learning to Live the Golden Rule to the best of her ability.

In 2009, Lara completed her certification and licensure and established a practice in TCM. From 2016 to 2021, Lara demonstrated alternative healing modalities in Introduction to Alternative & Complementary Medicine at Wichita State University.

In 2020, as with many people, the Covid-19 pandemic initiated a cascade of significant life changes. Lara's mom has been in Danny and Lara's care since 2015, and when the pandemic went global in the spring of 2020, Lara's strong intuition prompted her to close her office to stay home and care for her mom.

Lara's priorities have transformed as her commitment to the Course continues to deepen. She has felt Called to share the wisdom of *A Course in Miracles*, and *Together Is Home* is the first step in this next phase of her journey. Writing about the Course has been years in the making, yet she is certain that this is her pathway.

ACKNOWLEDGMENTS

M Y FIRST heart-spring of gratitude goes to the Holy Spirit. Spirit knows the entire plan of reconciliation and reunion, I do not. I am willing to do whatever is helpful—to do my part in the plan—but I do not know what actually is helpful. All I can do is follow inner guidance and just keep on following it. That is how this book has come about. It has been completely Spirit-led, and that is the only way I ever want it to be. Thank you, Holy Spirit. I trust You implicitly—You are my Guiding Light.

At the level of form, so much Loving support has been extended to this project. My husband, Danny Pollock, has provided unwavering encouragement every single day. His message since the beginning has been, "You do You—just keeping doing whatever it takes to accomplish your vision." I'm so thankful for his support, it means so much to me.

Our kids, Miranda, Brett and Tiger, and their amazing Dear Ones, have also held the space for me to follow this path, for they know this is my Calling. I delight in their independence, and I celebrate that the time is now right for me to write.

My mom, Greta W. Crosby, is an incredible human rights activist and wordsmith in her own right. As mentioned in the Preface, when I was pondering writing a book, yet feeling overwhelmed with the process, Mom gave me the nudge to see this project through. She has always viewed me with her adoring Mom-Goggles and that is a gift, indeed.

I also wish to posthumously acknowledge my dad, Robert Crosby. Though I was estranged from him for many years, the healing journey back to Love—seeing him for who truly he is—has been indescribably worthwhile. I am who I am because he is who he is.

You may recall that my best friend Kris has been mentioned several times in the book. I'd like to introduce Kristina Kirchmer, my best friend since 1979. She began studying *A Course in Miracles* with me in 2008, and I am so grateful to be able to share this learning journey together. What a great resource for feedback—my bestie, who knows me, and knows the Course, so well!

Appreciation goes to Dianne Waltner, who self-published her own book, *Evolving into Wholeness* in 2021. Her insights on the steps of self-publication helped pave the way for the manifestation of this book.

In the peer-review process, I thank Unity friends Joe Dunlavy and LeAnn Michalski for contributing wise and helpful input, greatly improving the book overall. In addition, both of my Study Groups have supported the on-going book-building process, generating ideas throughout its journey to fruition.

Rose Bromley, my mom's helper, has been my back-up during the many months of writing, editing, and preparing the book for self-publication. Rose has been a vital tag-team member, Lovingly caring for my mom and the household, allowing me to work on the book. There are no words to express my appreciation for everything she has done for our family.

Two more members of the family must be acknowledged for their loyal contribution to *Together Is Home*. Riley Rose Marie, our 13-year-old schnauzer, and Ava, our 6-year-old great dane, have provided constant companionship—lots of snuggles and warm fuzzies have gone into the making of this book.

A significant acknowledgement goes to Gary Renard, author of *The Disappearance of the Universe*, who changed the course of my life. His contribution to the world is inestimable. In addition, when I was seeking advice on who might edit *Together Is Home*, I reached out to Gary, inquiring if he might recommend a Course-knowledgeable editor. He promptly responded that the editor of *The Disappearance of the Universe*, D. Patrick Miller, was the best person for the job—and once again, I continue to heap on my gratitude for Gary's help.

When Gary recommended Patrick, I hadn't dared to dream that he might be able to help me with my book. Little did I know that his business, Fearless Literary, offers an entire array of services, facilitating every aspect of self-publication. An answer to a prayer, to be sure—Thank You, Holy Spirit, for guiding me once again. And Thank you Patrick, for your experienced input and patient support every step of the way!

Finally, a heartfelt 'Thank you' for anyone and everyone, family members, friends, friends of friends, neighbors, Course teachers and students, church members, clients, colleagues, fellow retreat participants, my dentist, my chiropractor, my cranio-sacral therapist, my former students, utility workers, even seatmates on airplanes, who have encouraged me along the way. Everybody needs encouragement. We have no idea how helpful it is when we tell another person, "Hey, more power to you! You can do this!" Thank you All, for your Loving support for the writing and publication of *Together Is Home*.